I0804698

“God’s Spirit ... doth persuade and enable us to embrace Jesus CHRIST, FREELY OFFERED to us in the gospel.”

Shorter Catechism Q. 31

Christ Freely Offered

A discussion of the general offer of salvation in the light of particular atonement

Christ Freely Offered

By Ken Stebbins

First published by Covenanter Press, 1978.

Tulip Publishing Edition, 2020.

For information contact:

Tulip Publishing, PO Box 3150, Lansvale, NSW, Australia 2166

www.tulippublishing.com.au

Book and Cover design by Tulip Publishing

PAPERBACK ISBN: 978–0–6487250–1–5

DIGITAL ISBN: 978–0–6487250–2–2

10 9 8 7 6 5 4 3 2 1

"Scripture tells us God works all things according to the counsel of his will (Eph. 1:11), and he does all his pleasure (Isa. 46:10). So is it proper to assume he delights in everything that happens—including the destruction of the wicked? Some would say yes. In fact, this is a notion that seems to be gaining influence in certain forums on the Internet. But God himself says he does not delight in the death of the wicked; he would rather see them repent (Eze. 18:23, 32; 33:11). How, then, do we reconcile God's sovereignty with his appeals to hardened sinners? Are we supposed to proclaim the gospel as a plea for sinners to be reconciled with God? Does the gospel message include a well-meant proffer of forgiveness and salvation to all sinners in general, or only the elect in particular? Some would say these are the hardest questions related to the sovereignty of God and the doctrine of election. Ken Stebbins tackles the conundrum and helps sort it out with great care, biblical precision, and uncommon clarity. This is the most readable, easy-to-follow work on the subject I know. It was a tremendous help to me 25 years ago when I was still fairly new to the doctrines of grace. I'm pleased to see it back in print."

Phil Johnson

Executive Director, Grace to You

"Ken Stebbins alerts us to the faulty steps in logic and the misreadings of Scripture that we can make when reflecting on God's eternal decree. The mystery is that God delights in the repentance and faith of lost men and women while not including them all in his eternal (decretive) will of salvation. But the author shows from Scripture and the history of theology that Jesus Christ can and should be sincerely and indiscriminately offered in the Gospel message. In the middle chapter there is a helpful defence of the doctrine of God's common grace that is germane to the subject. To those who are aware of the theological questions and who are looking for reliable answers we recommend this book."

Rev. Dr. Douglas Milne

Principal Emeritus, Presbyterian Theological College, Melbourne

"Calvinists are stewards of beautiful truths derived from Scripture. As such, we have the solemn responsibility to defend them from erroneous interpretation and application. *Christ Freely Offered* continues to be a helpful resource for those seeking a response against the Hyper-Calvinistic error that persists into our day. Especially helpful are the extensive and helpful discussions of major Reformed theologians on this issue."

Dr. Sam Waldron

President and Academic Dean,

Covenant Baptist Theological Seminary

To Eileen,
the love of my life and my companion
who has walked with me
and worked with me
and kept me warm
these 50 years

FOREWORD

The Reformed faith teaches, with the Bible, that God chooses a people whom He saves (Rom. 9:14–18; Eph. 1:3–11), yet He commands all and sundry to repent and believe the gospel (Matt. 11:28–30; Acts 17:30); He is in no way the author of sin (1 John 1:5), yet He is sovereign over evil (Isa. 45:7; Lam. 3:38); He does good to His enemies (Matt. 5:44–46), yet He is angry with the wicked every day (Psa. 7:11; 9:5). At first sight, it seems small wonder that the reader might seek refuge in the comfort that we see through the glass darkly (1 Cor. 13:12). A biblical equilibrium can be difficult to maintain, and the various responses often turn out to be flawed. 'Rabbi' Duncan's aphorism is often cited: "Hyper-Calvinism is all house and no door; Arminianism is all door and no house." And that is just the big picture; it leaves out a multitude of subtle and not-so-subtle variations.

A simple way into a difficult subject might be to cite Calvin himself on some biblical texts. On Romans 9:16–18, Calvin, while warning against idleness and inactivity, declares that "our election is to be attributed neither to our diligence, zeal, nor efforts, but is to be ascribed entirely to the counsel of God."[1] He refers the destruction of Pharaoh to "the just but secret counsel of God". Hence, "If this hardening of Pharaoh's heart is such as to be the cause of God's name being made known, it is blasphemous to accuse Him of any unrighteousness."[2] Verse 18 is stark, and Calvin does not back-peddle: "God favours with His mercy those whom He pleases according to His own will, and unsheaths the severity of His judgment against any person whom He pleases."[3]

Nevertheless, in Mark 10:21 it is said that Jesus loved the rich

1. John Calvin, *Commentary on Romans*, trans. Ross Mackenzie (Michigan: Eerdmans, 1995), 205 on Romans 9:16.
2. Calvin, *Romans*, 206, on Romans 9:17.
3. Calvin, *Romans*, 207.

young ruler who walked away sorrowful from Him. Some Reformed expositors have felt awkward about this, and the New American Standard even says that Jesus "felt a love" for the man—which is too weak, and not what the text says. Calvin does not resort to precarious explanations such as the rich young man must have been elect for Christ to love him or that Christ does not reveal the will of the Father. Instead, Calvin explained that "God is sometimes said to love those whom He does not approve or justify". Hence He loves political virtues even though they are not meritorious of salvation, but they do aid the preservation of the human race. The outward semblance of righteousness is of no avail for obtaining righteousness but it is not thereby to be rejected utterly. Christ can both love and hate at the same time: "It is not inconsistent, that the good seed, which God has implanted in some natures, shall be loved by Him, and yet that He should reject their persons and works on account of corruption".[4] The Reformer could speak of "the general benevolence of God, which extends to the whole human race".[5]

God can thus be said to love the reprobate in some non-saving sense. In addition, Calvin most emphatically taught human responsibility for sin: "So no one is really deceived unless he wants to be ... In short, men never come to grief except of their own choice."[6] This takes us to Calvin's treatment of Ezekiel 18:23 ("Have I any pleasure in the death of the wicked, declares the Lord God, and not rather that he should turn from his way and live?") Calvin deserves to be cited at length:

> God desires nothing more earnestly than that those who were perishing and rushing to destruction should return in the way of safety. And for this reason not only is the Gospel spread abroad in the world, but God wished to bear witness through all ages how inclined He is to pity. For although the heathen were destitute of the law and the prophets, yet they

---

4. John Calvin, *Commentary, Harmony of the Evangelists, Matthew, Mark and Luke*, trans. by William Pringle (Michigan: Baker Book House, 1979), 2:399 on Mark 10:21.
5. John Calvin, *Commentary on the Book of Psalms*, trans by James Anderson, (Grand Rapids: Baker, 1979), 2:154 on Psalm 44:3.
6. John Calvin, *Sermons on Titus*, trans. by Robert White (Edinburgh: Banner of Truth, 2015), 8.

were always endued with some taste of this doctrine. Truly enough they were suffocated by many errors: but we shall always find that they were induced by a secret impulse to seek for pardon, because this sense was in some way born with them, that God is to be appeased by all who seek Him ... In the Gospel we hear how familiarly He addresses us when He promises us pardon (Luke 1:78). And this is the knowledge of salvation to embrace His mercy which He offers us in Christ. It follows then, that what the prophet now says is very true, that God wills not the death of a sinner, because He meets him of His own accord, and is not only prepared to receive all who fly to His pity, but He calls them towards Him with a loud voice, when He sees how they are alienated from all hope of safety ...

We maintain that God does not will the death of sinners, since He equally calls all people to repentance and promises He is prepared to receive them if they only seriously repent. Some may object, saying that this would deny God's election, for He has predestined a fixed number to salvation. The prophet does not speak here of God's secret counsel, but only of God calling those in misery from despair that they may apprehend the hope of pardon, and repent and embrace the offer of salvation.

If anyone again objects, saying this proves that God acts with duplicity, the answer is ready: God always wishes the same thing, though by different ways, and in a manner we cannot understand. Although God's will is simple, yet it involves great variety, as far as our senses are concerned. It is not surprising that our eyes should be so blinded by intense light that we cannot judge with certainty how God wishes all to be saved and yet has devoted the reprobate to eternal destruction and wishes them to perish. While we now look through a glass darkly, we should be content with the measure of our own intelligence (1 Cor. 13:12). When we one day are like God and see Him face to face, then what is now obscure to us will become plain.[7]

7. John Calvin, *Commentary on the Prophet Ezekiel*, trans. by Thomas Myers, (Michigan: Baker, 1979), 2:246–249.

Calvin deeply resented the claim made by those he called "foul calumniators" that he made God the author of sin. God hardened Pharaoh's heart and Pharaoh hardened his own heart. In Calvin's explanation, "the hardness of heart is the sin of man, but the hardening of the heart is the judgment of God."[8] There are Calvinists who cannot live with a certain tension in their theological views, but Calvin was not of their ilk.

A number of issues are raised in all this. Christians are loved by God from before the foundation of the world, yet are children of wrath by nature (Eph. 1:4–5; 2:3–4). Even after a person becomes a believer, it is possible to speak of God's anger and hot displeasure against him/her (Psa. 6:1; 30:4–5; 38:1). Jesus grieved over those who rejected Him (Matt. 23:37). In Hosea 7:13 God declares: "I would redeem them, but they speak lies against me." Isaiah says: "the Lord longs to be gracious to you" (Isa. 30:18). In Judges we read that the Lord "became impatient over the misery of Israel" (ESV), or, as the NIV put it: "he could bear Israel's misery no longer" (Judges 10:16). The God of the Bible does not inflict suffering willingly, literally "from the heart" (Lam. 3:33). It is not something in which He takes delight. Indeed, His heart is churned up within Him at the thought of pouring out His anger on His sinful people (Hos. 11:8–9).

This means that in a sense, God both hates and loves sinners. To try to cast light on this, it is often said, even by someone as astute as Dr Martyn Lloyd-Jones, that "God hates the sin, but loves the sinner."[9] Augustine of Hippo too stated that a man "should not hate the person because of the fault, nor should he love the fault because of the person. He should hate the fault, but love the man."[10] This may all go back to Origen who declared that "those who are perfect will love the sinner but hate his sin".[11] There is much truth in this, but ultimately the sinner and his sin cannot be separated so easily. In any case, the Scripture says that God hates not just sin

8. John Calvin, *Commentary on the Four Last Books of Moses*, trans. by Charles William Bingham (Michigan: Baker, 1979), 1:141 on Exodus 7:3.
9. Martyn Lloyd-Jones, *Darkness and Light: An Exposition of Ephesians 4:17–5:17* (Edinburgh: Banner of Truth, 1982), 237.
10. Augustine, *City of God*, 14.6.
11. Gerald Bray, ed., *Ancient Christian Commentary on Scripture: Romans VI* (Illinois: IVP, 1998), 320.

but sinners (Psa. 5:5; 7:11; 11:5).

John Piper's *The Pleasures of God* has the theme: "His [God's] deeds are the overflow of his joy."[12] However, because Deuteronomy 28:63 says that "the Lord will rejoice over you to destroy you and bring you to nothing" and the three verses of Ezekiel 18:23, 32; 33:11 say God has no pleasure in the death of the wicked, Piper concludes: "The answer I propose is that God is grieved in one sense by the death of the wicked, and pleased in another."[13] We dare not go beyond Scripture, and place our understanding over and above God's Word. Not for nothing did Spurgeon complain about those who applied "grammatical gunpowder" to texts, in order to deny their obvious meaning.[14]

This Foreword began with references to Calvin, and it may be best to conclude the same way. In his commentary on John 17:23 where Christ speaks of the Father loving Christians even as He loves His Son, Calvin says: "Thus we are at the same time the enemies and the friends of God, until, atonement having been made for our sins, we are restored to favour with God."[15] We are all in need of help in this area of how to offer Christ freely to all and sundry without undermining the sufficiency of Christ's atonement for His people. Ken Stebbins proves to be a clear and lucid guide.

Peter Barnes,
Minister at Revesby Presbyterian, Sydney
August 2020

12. John Piper, *The Pleasures of God* (Oregon: Multnomah, 1991), 50.
13. Piper, *The Pleasures of God*, 66.
14. Cited in Iain H. Murray, *Spurgeon v. Hyper-Calvinism: The Battle for Gospel Preaching* (Edinburgh: Banner of Truth, 1995), 150–1.
15. John Calvin, *Commentary on John*, trans. by William Pringle (Michigan: Baker, 1979), 186.

PREFACE TO THIRD EDITION

I am grateful to Brett and Lucy Lee-Price, of Tulip Publishing, for their encouragement to put *Christ Freely Offered* back on the market.

It is more than 45 years since I first wrote this book. The denomination I was part of at the time was debating the topic and asked me to follow it up, having previously expressed an interest in, and raised my concerns for, the issues at stake. That was back in 1974. We were not long married, our first child was on the way, and in the middle of it all, over many months, I researched and wrote this book. A big thank you to my longsuffering wife.

Since then the landscape of the evangelical church has changed dramatically. There are many other challenges that face us today. But there are many things that haven't changed, the most important being the blessed gospel of our wonderful Saviour, Jesus Christ.

At the beginning of my ministry I wrote from the viewpoint of what I believed from the Word of God, but with limited experience in preaching. Now, after more than 40 years in the ministry and having proved the truth by experience of what I wrote back then, I am more than ever convinced that the gospel is God's only "power to salvation" (Rom. 1:16), and of the great need to plead with sinners perishing in their sins to repent and turn to an all-sufficient Saviour. Woe to that man who preaches any other gospel (Gal. 1:6–10) or who confuses the distinctive message God has given us to proclaim (1 Cor. 14:8).

Over this time I have also been greatly blessed to prove the truth of the free offer of the gospel through the experience of others, especially in reading more widely as to what God has done in pouring out His Spirit in times of genuine revival. It has warmed my heart and encouraged me in the ministry to read of men who were obviously committed to the Reformed faith so blessed in their preaching in the power of the Holy Spirit. It is my prayer that God would be gracious and would yet visit us again in this way.

In this latest edition I have made no substantial changes to what I originally wrote: I don't believe the issues have changed. There are a few minor corrections, and, in view of renewed interest in the "Marrow Controversy" in recent years, I have sought to deal with matters surrounding that period in a more thoughtful and nuanced way.

I am very thankful that, if I go to my grave only ever having written one book, in the providence of God it is on this topic that is so very dear to my heart.

Soli Deo gloria

Ken Stebbins
Brisbane
April 2020

INTRODUCTION

This book discusses the free offer of the gospel in the light of particular atonement. The doctrine of particular atonement is not in question and little can be added to the works of Owen, Smeaton and others.

The subtitle refers to the atonement to distinguish this discussion from what is normally called the Hyper-Calvinist controversy, in which the free offer is denied on the grounds of man's inability.

The present debate centres around the question of whether God offers salvation to every hearer of the gospel, and if so, how such an offer can be sincere in the light of particular atonement.

No one in this debate denies that the gospel is to be preached promiscuously. The issue is not whether to preach the gospel, but what gospel to preach.

The implications of the "free offer" or "well-meant offer" can be summed up in three questions:

1. **Does God desire the salvation of everyone?**
2. **Does God offer the gospel to all because He loves all? Does He love all?**
3. **Does God offer Christ and salvation to everyone in the preaching of the gospel?**

These three questions are put to us by Rev. David Engelsma of the Protestant Reformed Church (USA).[1] This book is an answer to

1. David Engelsma, "Our Protestant Reformed Position Regarding the 'Free Offer of the Gospel'", *Standard Bearer*, 1st November 1973; 15th December, 1973. His articles are a defence of the Protestant Reformed Church's rejection of a "Free Offer". These three questions arise from Rev. David Engelsma's summing up of the "Free Offer" issue.

those questions.

I approach each question in turn and examine it in the light of Scripture and in the light of the history of theology. Only Scripture will provide us with a source of infallible knowledge. However in the history of theology, Bible-believing men on both sides have drawn from the resources of Scripture and arrived at different positions with regard to the "free offer". It would therefore be foolish to pass by the insights of such well-meaning pioneers with a pious, "Let's get back to the Bible". Historical positions must be reviewed if for no other reason than to discover unanswered questions in one's own "Biblical" view.

If at one time I quote our Reformed fathers with approval, it is not because I believe they were infallible, but because I believe their writings sum up the teaching of Scripture.

If at another time I seem overly-critical, it is not from contempt or because I think I have greater inspiration, but only because I sincerely believe the position espoused is either unscriptural or inconsistent. Sometimes our earlier fathers used loose or inappropriate phrases and it was only the rise of heresy that "gave occasion to more diligence of search and wariness of expression than had formerly been used by some".[2] There were others that overreacted against heresy and, in an endeavour to silence the heretic, muzzled the voice of truth as well.

I have tried in this book to stick with the present issues and avoid incidental doctrines. Other questions are touched upon only in so far as they affect the free offer.

- No attempt is made to answer the **problem of sin.** Basically this book proceeds from an infralapsarian position of assuming a decree of sin and going from there.
- No attempt is made to prove **particular atonement.** As was said before there is little that can be added to the works of others.
- The question of **common grace** is touched upon only

2. John Owen, *The Death of Death in the Death of Christ* (London: Banner of Truth, 1963), 311.

> in so far as it affects God's attitude in making an offer to individual men. The implications of common grace as a basis for secular culture are properly the subject of a separate paper.

Finally I personally testify that I trembled in attempting to understand the nature of God and His decrees. God indeed is knowable but who will dare to try and understand beyond what the Scriptures teach?

"He who would be a rash man indeed who should flatter his readers that he was about to furnish an exhaustive explanation of this mystery of the divine will. But any man who can contribute his mite to a more satisfying and consistent exposition of the Scripture's bearing on it is doing a good service to truth" (R. L. Dabney).[3]

K. W. Stebbins
Wollongong
6th December 1975

3. R. L. Dabney, "God's Indiscriminate Proposals of Mercy", *Discussions: Evangelical and Theological* (London: Banner of Truth, 1967), 1:309.

CONTENTS

Chapter One

GOD'S DELIGHT THAT ALL BE SAVED

Having outlined in the Introduction, the three questions to be considered, in this chapter I wish to examine the first question arising from Engelsma's summing up: Does God desire the salvation of everyone?

1. The Relation between God's Nature and His Will

Revealed and Decretive Will

We must first consider what is meant when we speak of the will of God. Here is introduced the distinction between God's revealed will and His decretive will. This is not an arbitrary or inadmissible distinction, but reflects as nearly as possible the teaching of Scripture.

That some such distinction must be made is apparent if we are rightly to divide the Word of Truth. Even Arminians and Lutherans, who object to the Reformed distinction, postulate an antecedent and consequent, or absolute and conditional will.[1]

Reformed theologians have tried to express the distinction in various ways:

i. The <u>secret</u> and <u>revealed</u> will of God (<u>*voluntas arcana*</u> and <u>*voluntas revelata*</u>). "This is the most common distinction... [it] is based on Deut. 29:29. The former is the will of God's decree, which is largely hidden in God, while the latter is the will of the precept, which is revealed in the law and the gospel."[2] The idea of "decree" is not explicit in the word "secret" and this concept is more precisely expressed as:

1. Charles Hodge, *Systematic Theology* (London: James Clark and co., 1960), 1:404; William Cunningham, *Historical Theology* (London: Banner of Truth, 1969), 2:454.
2. Louis Berkhof, *Systematic Theology* (Grand Rapids: Eerdmans, 1968), 77.

ii. The decretive and preceptive will of God (or decretive and legislative will).[3]

iii. *Voluntas beneplaciti* and *voluntas signi*. The former refers to God's decrees founded upon His good pleasure; the latter to the precepts of God, as well as events in the world inasmuch as they are all signs of His will.[4] This is a happy distinction in that it brings out the essential unity of the will of God. The basis of that will is the good pleasure of God. The decree is then God's purpose arising from His good pleasure. If we seek an insight into what God's good pleasure is, we will find it in His precepts and in the way God works out His decree. There is, of course, no guarantee that our insights, especially if they are based upon the *signa* of events in the world, will be infallibly correct.

iv. The will of God's purpose and the will of God's delight (or, will of good pleasure and will of complacency; or, will of *eudokia* and will of *euarestia*).[5] This too is a useful distinction. By it theologians meant to point out that God's precepts are a reliable witness to what God delights in, whereas world events (which reveal only the bare purpose of His decree) must first be interpreted aright before we can deduce what it is that God delights in.

Each pair outlined above is subtly different from the others, but all are reasonable and valid distinctions to apply in understanding the will of God.

We are not suggesting that there are two wills in God. What we are doing is trying to express two ideas by means of the same word "will". "When we speak of the decretive and preceptive will of God, we are using the word 'will' in two different senses. By the former God has determined what He will do or what shall come to pass; in the latter He reveals to us what we are in duty bound to do."[6]

Nonetheless, while we realise that we are talking about two

---

3. Berkhof, 77.
4. John Owen, "A Display of Arminianism", *Works of John Owen* (London: Banner of Truth, 1967), 10:45; Berkhof, *Systematic Theology*, 77.
5. Berkhof, 77.
6. Berkhof, 79.

God's nature as the source of God's will

different concepts, they are related concepts. Owen goes too far when he says "we must exactly distinguish between man's duty and God's purpose, there being no connection between them".[7]

Of course there is a connection between them, because both are expressions of the character of God. The common fountain of both God's revealed will and His decretive will are the principles or attributes that constitute His character.[8] These attributes are necessary because God is God, but their manifestation in the revealed and decretive will are free acts of God. That is, while God cannot act against Himself, when He does act, He is perfectly free to manifest or express Himself in any way that accords with His attributes.

There are then three starting points for understanding God's nature: His revealed will, His decretive will and direct revelation.

God's **revealed will** is a reliable witness to God's attributes. When God says *"You shalt not bear false witness"* (Exod. 20:16) we may legitimately deduce that the whole of God's character abhors falsehood.

God may also reveal this truth about His attributes through **direct revelation** as in *"The Lord hates a lying tongue"* (Prov. 6:16*f*). The former command of Exodus 20 is an expression of, and a reliable witness to, this principle in God which is directly

7. John Owen, *The Death of Death*, 187.
8. By "attributes" I mean the perfections or properties of God that constitute His nature. This is not to deny His unity or simplicity. It is true that "God's essence and perfections are not distinct", but are "identical with His Being" (Berkhof, *Systematic Theology*, 62). Distinctions, however, aid our understanding and are legitimate on the grounds of Scriptural usage. I use the term "principle" in a less comprehensive sense, to refer to any one aspect of any of God's attributes, e.g. We might express God's attribute of righteousness in terms of a number of principles; such as a principle by which He hates lying, another by which He hates murder, another by which He loves uprightness etc.

revealed in Proverbs 6.

However we may not deduce from world events (i.e. the outworking of His **decree**) infallible knowledge of God's attributes. We could not, for instance, take the example of Jacob, who was a liar and deceiver and presume that God delights in liars because He favoured Jacob and not Esau.

The only reliable interpretation of world events as an expression of the character of God is the Word of God, i.e. the revealed will must interpret the decretive will. The decretive will is not an infallible guide to the nature and character of God. If we wish to discover this, we must see what God has revealed directly or through His precepts. "The light of God's revelation is necessary for the interpretation of His providential guidances."[9]

God's good pleasure

The basis of God's will—decreed and revealed—is the character of God. We might also say that the basis of God's will is His good pleasure. According as God delights in something or abhors something, so He commands or forbids it, and so He determines what shall be His decree.

But we need to discern when God's "pleasure" (as used in the Bible) means His delight and when it expresses nothing more than bare purpose. Shedd puts it this way: "The 'good pleasure' (εὐδοκία), in accordance with which God permits sin, must not be confounded with the pleasure or complacency (ἀγάπη), in accordance with which He promulgates the moral law forbidding sin. The term 'good pleasure' has the meaning of 'pleasure' in the phrase, 'Be pleased, or please to do me this favour.' All that is asked for is a **decision** to do the favour."[10]

When "pleasure" means "delight" or "complacency" it refers to God's nature i.e. God's principles. When "pleasure" means nothing more than bare purpose, it refers to God's decree. God may or may not delight in the actual event that performs His decree, even

9. Berkhof, *Systematic Theology*, 536. Of course, some of God's precepts are a plainer witness to His attributes than others. *"You shalt not bear false witness"* testifies immediately to the veracity of God. The precepts of the ceremonial law, though, are not as plain a witness and must be interpreted through such faith and knowledge as eg. the writer of Hebrews possessed. They then tell us much about God.

10. W.G.T. Shedd, *Dogmatic Theology* (Minneapolis: Klock & Klock, 1979), 1:407.

though He will certainly delight in the purpose that the event achieves. There are many examples in Scripture where "pleasure" means no more than "purpose".

Isa. 53:10, *"It pleased (Heb. chaphets[11]) the Lord to bruise him."* This refers to God's bare purpose. The Father took no delight in seeing *"Herod, and Pontius Pilate, with the Gentiles, and the people of Israel doing whatsoever His hand and His counsel determined before to be done"* (*cf* Acts 4:27–29). He may well have taken delight in the purpose achieved: the salvation of men and women. But He took no delight in the sin itself.

Prov. 21:1, *"The king's heart is in the hand of the Lord, as the rivers of water: He turns it wherever He will"* (Heb. chaphets). Here God's good pleasure is simply rendered as His "will".

Both God's nature and His decree are implied in Psalm 115:3 *"Our God is in the heavens. He does whatever He pleases"* (Heb. chaphets). This verse refers primarily to God's decree, but also looks behind the decree to the principles in which He delights.

In the New Testament "good pleasure", as nothing more than God's decretive will, is expressed by the word Greek word, *eudokia*.

Matt. 11:25–26, *"I thank You, Father, Lord of heaven and earth, that You have hidden these things from the wise and prudent and have revealed them to babes. Even so, Father, for so it seemed good* (εὐδοκία) *Your sight."*

In Ephesians 1:9 the latent meaning of "delight" is there: *"... having made known to us the mystery of His will, according to His good pleasure* (εὐδοκία) *which He purposed in Himself"*—the primary sense, though, is that of God's purpose.

There are other examples in Scripture when "pleasure" can only mean "delight":

Psa. 5:4, *"You are not a God who takes pleasure* (Heb. chaphets) *in wickedness."* This cannot very well mean that God has no decree of, or purpose in, wickedness. God had a very righteous purpose to perform, as in the case of Pharaoh (Rom. 9:17). But He takes no pleasure in the wickedness of Pharaoh itself.

11. For convenience I will use a modified Strong's transliteration.

Again God complains against Israel that they *"chose that in which I do not delight* (Heb. chaphets)*"* (Isa. 65:12, 66:4). God's "delight" (in this case "non-delight", or "abhorrence") is not His decree or purpose, but a principle in His very nature.

The same thought is expressed in Jeremiah 19:5 where Israel committed idolatry, things *"which I did not command or speak, nor did it come into My mind"* (Heb. *leb,* lit. "heart"). Here the close connection between God's precepts and His attributes is apparent. Idolatry is completely abhorrent to the mind of God—a thing which Israel should have known from the precept which God *"commanded"* and *"spoke"*, even though He permitted it by His decree.

Ezekiel passages In the light of the above let us now turn to those contentious verses in Ezekiel:

"'Do I have any pleasure (Heb. chaphets) *at all that the wicked should die?' says the Lord God, 'and not that he should turn from his ways and live?'"* (18:23)

"'Why should you die, O house of Israel? For I have no pleasure (Heb. chaphets) *in the death of one who dies,' says the Lord God. 'Therefore turn and live!'"* (18:31-32)

"'As I live,' says the Lord God, 'I have no pleasure (Heb. chaphets) *in the death of the wicked, but that the wicked turn from his way and live. Turn, turn from your evil ways! For why should you die, O house of Israel?'"* (33:11)

These verses state God's revealed will—i.e. His command to *"turn and live".* We could quite legitimately deduce on this basis alone that it was therefore God's nature to delight in men turning to Him and His abhorrence that they die.

The principle of delight is that men should turn and live. The principle of abhorrence is that men should continue in their sin and die.

This is not just a delight or abhorrence in "things" abstracted from the person, as Owen seems to suggest.[12] God's delight

12. John Owen, *The Death of Death*, 200: "His *promises*, indeed, as *particularly* applied, hold out His mind to the *persons* to whom they are applied; but as *indefinitely* proposed, they reveal no other intention of God but what we before

Delight in person and thing together

would be not just in repentance and faith as things in themselves—but in the wicked themselves repenting and believing. (This is **not** the same as saying He actually desires their salvation as we shall see later). Similarly His abhorrence would be not just in the concept of death. His abhorrence would be in the death of the wicked himself.

God may indeed delight to see His righteousness vindicated and His justice manifested in the death of the wicked. But He takes no delight in his actual death.

This would seem to be the plain and consistent meaning of the passages in Ezekiel. To say that God's delight is just in "things" and not in "persons performing those things" does not do justice to those passages.

Delight in non-events

Some will ask how God can say He "would have" delight in what will never come to pass. First God's "delight" refers to God's nature, not the expression of that delight when an event occurs. God's nature is God's nature whether anything happens or not.

Secondly even in the non-occurrence of the event God's nature is expressed. Because of His simplicity and unity, all His attributes or principles are one. The same principle which expresses "delight" when the wicked repent, expresses "abhorrence" (or "non-delight") when the wicked die. It is the same principle that expresses itself according to outward circumstances.[13]

It is therefore quite legitimate to say that God delights that the wicked would turn to Him, even if they never do. To express non-delight at an event implies that delight would have been expressed if the event were not to have taken place.

Unity of God's principles in all His actions

The unity of God's principles may also shed

---

discovered, which concerns *things*, not *persons*, even his determinate purpose infallibly to connect faith and salvation".

13. A good example of how two opposite manifestations represent one principle is God's delighting in righteousness and showing wrath at wickedness. "Delight" and "wrath" do not imply two opposite principles as their sources, but a single attribute of righteousness manifesting itself in a way that accords with contingent circumstances.

light on a piece of well-worn *Protestant Reformed* logic. First though let us see how, by examining those principles of God's nature and their free expression in His revealed and decretive will, we may understand better the character of God.

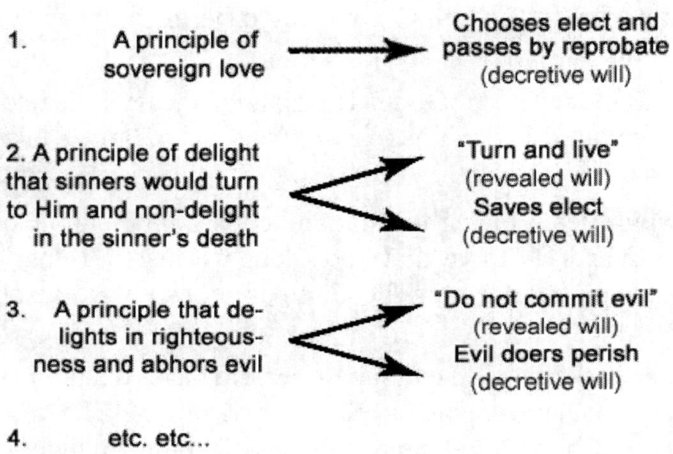

See note.[14]

To have a proper understanding of the character of God we have to hold in view all those principles of His nature.

Now the Protestant Reformed Church bases its arguments on the following "logic":

- The reprobate is the object of God's hatred.
- Because of God's hatred the reprobate is doomed.
- How can it be said that God desires the salvation of the reprobate?

Admittedly the word "desire" is not a happy one. But might it not

14. I use the term "principle" and not the term "reason". God certainly had a reason (unknown to us) for choosing those who are the elect and passing by the rest. My purpose is not to identify God's reasons or motives for acting, but to show that, when God acts, He is expressing the principles of His nature. To equate "reason" with "principle" in the above would be to destroy the freedom of God's actions and make them as necessary as His nature.

also be asked—how can God delight that the reprobate would turn and be saved?

The solution lies partly in the unity of the principles which make up the character of God. It is wrong to imagine that the principles which God expresses in His dealings with the elect have nothing to do with those that He expresses in His dealings with the reprobate. Why should those principles in 2. and 3. above be mutually exclusive—as though God is of one nature at one time, and another at another?

If God by His very nature delights in righteousness and therefore the reprobate, because of his sin, is an object of God's hatred—does that exclude God from taking no delight in his death and finding it abhorrent? Are not both principles actively present in God?

Likewise, God by His very nature, delights that the sinner would turn to Him. But can He lay aside His principle of righteousness? Of course not. He still views the unregenerate sinner with abhorrence —even the elect who are objects of His electing love.

None of God's attributes should be isolated. To exalt His righteousness at the expense of His abhorrence at the sinner's death, or His abhorrence at the sinner's death at the expense of His righteousness will lead to a distorted view of God. Or to conceive of God in both aspects—but to think of only one when considering the elect and of only the other when considering the reprobate will lead to the worship of a schizophrenic deity.

"Desire" or "Delight"

One final point needs to be made concerning the use of the word "desire". As we shall see it is a word that has been quite commonly used by nearly all Reformed Theologians from Calvin down to the present day.

Murray and Stonehouse admit that "the word *desire* has come to be used in the debate, not because it is necessarily the most accurate or felicitous word but because it serves to set forth quite sharply a certain implication of the full and free offer of the Gospel to all.... The word *desire* has been used in order to express the thought epitomised in Ezekiel 33:11, which is to the effect that God has pleasure that the wicked turn from his evil way and live. It might as well have been said 'It pleases God that the wicked repent and be saved."[15]

It not only "might as well have been said"—it would have been said a whole lot better. The word "desire" does nothing to clarify the issues when discussing the verse in the framework of an exact theology.

"To desire" has both constitutional and volitional overtones. It implies, not only a "delight in" (constitutional), but a positive "wish" or "will" (volitional). As such, the term is confusing, since we have seen that the Ezekiel passages speak of God's "delight" as that which constitutes His nature, apart from, and prior to, any consideration of decreeing or commanding. God's "delight" refers to the very character of God; but "desire" speaks not so much of His character, as of the volitional expression of that character.

One is forced to ask—what volitional expression? Patently not the decree of God, since then it would only include the elect and say nothing of the reprobate concerning whom the Ezekiel passages most certainly also speak.

Equally obvious is the fact that God's revealed will cannot be meant. For then all Ezekiel 18:32 says is: *"I command you to turn: **wherefore** I command you to turn and live."*

But if God's "delight" refers merely to God's nature, this verse makes sense, i.e. "It is not My nature to delight in your death: **wherefore** I command you to turn and live."

In the light of the above it would seem far better to avoid the "volitional" aspect of "desire" altogether and be satisfied with the word "delight" which I think adequately expresses the idea of Ezekiel and other passages we will consider later.

Summary

To summarise then we state that God delights that men would turn to Him because of His very nature. His delight is not a free act of will but a necessary principle in God.

But as to how He will express this delight He is perfectly free. He

15. John Murray and Ned Stonehouse, *The Free Offer of the Gospel* (Phillipsburg, NJ: Presbyterian & Reformed Publishing, 1949), 4.

may do so in any way that is consistent with the other principles that constitute His nature. As it is, He expresses this particular principle in His command that all should turn to Him (His revealed will) and in His converting the elect (His decretive will) whom He has chosen for reasons known only to Himself.

That He then condemns the reprobate is in no way contrary to that principle by which He delights that men would turn to Him and by which He abhors the death of the sinner. The reason for the sinner's condemnation is his own sin against which God reveals His wrath—as He is bound to because His nature includes that principle by which He delights in righteousness and justice. This latter principle by no means contradicts, but only complements, the other principles of God's nature.

It is God's nature in unity that is the fountain of God's decree. Thereby the whole of God's character delights in the whole of His purpose. But the individual means God uses may indeed give Him no pleasure as is patent in Isaiah 65:12, 66:4 and Jeremiah 19:5.

Both Arminian and Hyper-Calvinist err by refusing to recognise this. One says "God must delight in every detail of His decree; therefore He does not decree the reprobate's doom". The other says "God must delight in every detail of His decree; therefore He delights in the reprobate's doom".

Each has made his bed.

2. Historical Survey

John Calvin tackles the whole subject of the will of God with fierce boldness and extreme caution. His contention is that we are to be

John Calvin

completely bold and assert that to find the cause of all things "we must always return to the mere pleasure of the divine will, the cause of which is hidden in Himself"[16]. This is God's secret will, the cause of which is His good pleasure. "But if you proceed farther to ask why He pleased, you ask for something greater and more sublime than the will of God, and nothing can be found."[17]

16. John Calvin, *Institutes of Christian Religion*, 3.23.4.
17. Calvin, *Institutes*, 3.23.2.

Calvin sets himself definite limits. We can barely penetrate the secret counsel of God. "I do not accede to the demand to investigate what God wills to hide far from inquisitive curiosity."[18]

He draws a distinction between the secret will of God and that will "of which voluntary obedience is the counterpart"[19] or God's "precept"[20], though his terminology is not as precise as later Reformed teaching. Using Deuteronomy 29:29 he says: "We see how he exhorts the people to study the doctrine of the law in accordance with a heavenly decree, because God has been pleased to promulgate it, while He at the same time confines them within boundaries, for the simple reason that it is not lawful for men to pry into the secret things of God."[21]

Having thus warned men to exercise caution in "prying into the secret things of God" he proceeds to enjoin them to concentrate on God's revealed will if they are to discover their duty. However for Calvin, God's revealed will reveals not only what is man's duty, but also "what is pleasing to God".[22]

Conversely, God's secret will is not always, in the event itself, pleasing to God. Concerning Absalom he writes: "So far as Absalom's crime is a monstrous impiety against his father, a perfidious violation of a wife and a profanation of the order of nature, it certainly is displeasing to God; for He takes pleasure in honesty, chastity, good faith and modesty, and it is this order that He prescribes and wills to be obeyed and observed unimpaired among men. But because He is pleased to avenge the adultery of David in this way, He wills in the same way things that seem different to us."[23] He thus balances God's non-delight in a sin which is decreed against His delight in the purposes such a sin achieves.

Despite all this Calvin does little else to reconcile God's revealed will with His secret will. "While in Himself the will is

18. John Calvin, *Concerning the Eternal Predestination of God* (London: James Clark and Co., 1961), 183.
19. Calvin, *Institutes*, 3.20.43.
20. Calvin, *Institutes*, 1.18.4.
21. Calvin, *Institutes*, 3.21.3.
22. Calvin, *Institutes*, 1.17.3.
23. Calvin, *Eternal Predestination*, 184.

one and undivided, to us it appears manifold, because, from the feebleness of our intellect, we cannot comprehend how though after a different manner, He wills and wills not the very same thing."[24] Calvin is satisfied simply to accept that the wisdom of God appears to be "manifold" or "multiform".[25] This may be so, but it hardly clarifies anything.

Calvin also explains this apparent contrariety in God in terms of an anthropomorphism.[26] When God expresses a will that all men would turn to Him (eg. Matt. 23:37) He is speaking anthropomorphically, in terms of "human affections". Again this may be so but it is not an explanation. Anthropomorphisms, to be of any use, must indicate in what direction the real solution lies. When we speak of God's "hands spread out all the day" we understand by this God's power to act. Similarly God's "eyes" speak of His power to perceive. God's "repentance" of His change in relationship to man. Such terms are used to convey, quickly and concretely, a very definite idea. But to speak of God's "desire to save all" (and Calvin does) as an anthropomorphism, and to leave it at that, says next to nothing.

It is interesting to see how Calvin handles the Ezekiel passages which we have previously expounded. When defending predestination against Pighius he explains God's will that all men live as a bare invitation.[27]

However in his *Institutes* he goes further, though again he is very cautious. Concerning Ezekiel 18:23 he writes: "God is undoubtedly ready to pardon whenever the sinner turns. Therefore He does not will his death in so far as He wills his repentance. But experience shows that this will for the repentance of those whom He invites to Himself is not such as to make Him touch all their hearts. Still it cannot be said that He acts deceitfully; for though the external word only renders those who hear it, and do not obey it, inexcusable, it is still truly regarded as an evidence of the grace by which He reconciles men to Himself. Let us therefore hold the doctrine of the prophet, that God has no pleasure in the death of the sinner:

24. Calvin, *Institutes*, 1.18.3.
25. Calvin, *Institutes*, 1.18.3 c.f. 3.24.17.
26. Calvin, *Institutes*, 3.24.17.
27. Calvin, *Eternal Predestination*, 106.

that the godly may feel confident that whenever they repent God is ready to pardon them; and that the wicked may feel that their guilt is doubled, when they respond not to the great mercy and condescension of God."[28] He thus speaks of God's readiness to forgive even the reprobate, who, by despising such a disposition on God's part, increases his own guilt.

In his pulpit preaching though, Calvin was swept off his feet by the force of the prophet's message: "God **desires** nothing more earnestly than that those who were perishing and rushing to destruction should return into the way of safety. And for this reason not only is the gospel spread abroad in the world, but God wished to bear witness through all ages how He is inclined to pity. For, although the heathen were destitute of the law and the prophets, yet they were always endued with some taste of this doctrine."[29]

But how shall we reconcile this with the fact that God does indeed "wish" (i.e. decree) the death of the wicked? Calvin says "the knot is easily untied" (I love how Calvin throws in expressions like this): "God always wishes the same thing, though by different ways, and in a manner inscrutable to us"; and "there is no absurdity in God's undertaking a twofold character, not that He is two-faced Himself... but because His counsels are incomprehensible to us." Is then God chargeable with duplicity? By no means, "though He takes up a twofold character because this was necessary for our comprehension."[30]

Finally Calvin appeals to Deuteronomy 29:29. Although it can be quite certainly stated that God "is not delighted by the death of him who perishes" yet the import of the prophet's message is not to "dispute with subtlety about His incomprehensible plans, but... to keep our attention close to God's word". "Hence let us leave to God His own secrets, and exercise ourselves as far as we can in the law, in which God's will is made plain to us and to our children."[31]

It would seem that for Calvin "truth lay not in this extreme or

28. Calvin, *Institutes*, 3.24.15.
29. John Calvin, *Commentary on the First Twenty Chapters of the Book of the Prophet Ezekiel* (Edinburgh: Calvin Translation Society, 1850), 2:246,267.
30. Calvin, *Ezekiel*, 247.
31. Calvin, *Ezekiel*, 267.

that extreme, nor somewhere in between, but in both truths held in both extremes". It would be impossible for instance to label Calvin as either supralapsarian or infralapsarian. Sometimes he is blatantly supralapsarian as when he says "we can have no reason for God's reprobating men but His will"[32] and at other times he is just as plainly infralapsarian: "though their perdition depends on the predestination of God, the cause of it is in themselves".[33]

In like manner Calvin maintains to its fullness that God desires earnestly the repentance and salvation of the reprobate, while at the same time realising that God must wish the death of the reprobate. If we seek a further explanation Calvin says, "The knot is easily untied—God's will is inscrutable".

Such language is not only frustrating, it also leaves much to be desired if it is to clarify and not cloud the issue. Nonetheless, Calvin is a whole lot closer to the truth than anyone who, for the sake of a simple watertight system, simply rejects what he cannot reconcile.

The Synod of Dort

The Canons of Dort are undeniably infralapsarian in character[34] and speak of God "passing by" or "leaving" the reprobate in the "common misery into which they have wilfully plunged themselves". Therefore problems that go back to the ultimate reason in the mind of God for allowing this state to occur when He delights not in the death of the wicked do not arise.

The doctrine that "God, by a mere arbitrary act of His will, without the least respect or view to any sin, has predestinated the greatest part of the world to eternal damnation, and has created them for this very purpose", the Reformed Churches "not only do not acknowledge, but even detest with their whole soul."[35]

Dort saw nothing incongruous in God abhorring some of the means He has foreordained to achieve His purpose. The sins of the saints "very highly offend God" and "grieve the Holy Spirit".[36]

---

32. Calvin, *Institutes*, 3.22.11.
33. Calvin, *Institutes*, 3.23.8.
34. Canons of Dort, 1.5, 1.6, 1.15, 3 & 4.9.
35. Canons of Dort, Conclusion.
36. Canons of Dort, 5.5.

Article 8, Heads 3 & 4 is often quoted in connection with the free offer: "As many as are called by the gospel are unfeignedly called. For God has most earnestly and truly in His Word declared what is acceptable to Him, namely that those who are called should come to Him. He also seriously promises rest of soul and eternal life to all who come to Him and believe."

This only expresses what Ezekiel prophesied, namely: that it is acceptable to God (His delight) that all who hear the gospel (reprobate and elect) should come to Him. Engelsma tries to get around this by saying that it is only "the activity of coming to Christ that is pleasing to God".[37] But Article 8 says more than this—it says that it is acceptable that all hearers themselves come to God.

In fact H. C. Hoeksema recognises that Dort was talking about "persons" and not "things". He tries a different tack. He reinterprets "it is pleasing to God that those who are called should come" as "simply meaning that it is right in God's sight that men should heed the call to faith and repentance".[38] This again is not what the Article says. It is not just talking about what is right and wrong, but what is pleasing (Lat. *gratum*) to God concerning each particular person to whom the gospel is preached.

Westminster Confession

The language of the Westminster Confession is also infralapsarian. "The rest of mankind, God was pleased, according to the unsearchable counsel of His own will, whereby He extends or withholds mercy as He pleases, for the glory of His sovereign power over His creatures, to pass by and to ordain them to dishonour and wrath for their sin, to the praise of His glorious justice."[39] This section speaks of preterition ("passed by"), which is sovereign ("pleased, according to the unsearchable counsel of His will"), and precondemnation ("ordain to dishonour and wrath") which is purely judicial ("for their sin").

Like the Canons, the Confession posits the ground for the

37. David Engelsma, "Our Protestant Reformed Position Regarding the 'Free Offer of the Gospel'", *Standard Bearer*, 1st November 1973, 15th December, 1973.
38. Homer C. Hoeksema, "The O.P.C. and the 'Free Offer'" *Standard Bearer*, 15th December, 1973.
39. WCF 3.7.

reprobate's condemnation in foreordained sin. There has to be a reason for punishment. There need be no reason for grace.

Something must be said about foreordination to wrath as an eternal decree. This should not be necessary, but Runia and others have, of late, queried "the pre-temporal nature of the divine counsel".[40]

Precondemnation is judicial in the sense that it is the necessary consequence of another decree—foreordination to sin. Both decrees are eternal. God did not "happen" to find men sinful, and therefore "had" to punish. But precondemnation is judicial in that, once God had foreordained sin, He necessarily ordained judgment. John Murray says: "The ground of dishonour and wrath is sin alone. But the reason why the non-elect are ordained to this dishonour and wrath when others, the elect, are not is sovereign differentiation on God's part and there is no other answer to the question."[41]

Beyond this the Confession does not go. It leaves unanswered the question as to why God permitted sin and does not try and reconcile how God who delights neither in sin nor its consequences could have decreed both.

Francis Turretin

Francis Turretin was a leading theologian and defender of Calvinistic orthodoxy in the 17th century and one of the authors of the *Formula Consensus Helvetica* (*qv.*), the Confession drawn up by the Swiss Reformed churches to counter Amyraldianism and to defend the verbal inspiration of the Bible. His *Institutes of Elenctic Theology* was "widely used as a textbook, up to its use at Princeton Theological Seminary by the Princeton theologians only to be replaced by Charles Hodge's *Systematic Theology* in the late 19th century."[42]

In his Institutes, Turretin writes: "...God delights in the conversion and life of the sinner, as a thing pleasing in itself, and congruous

40. Peter DeJong, *Crisis in the Reformed Churches* (Grand Rapids: Reformed Fellowship, 1968), 178.
41. DeJong, *Crisis*, 155.
42. When I was researching this book, Turretin's *Institutes* was still only available in Latin. I found a copy in one of the leading theological seminaries in Sydney. I had to cut every second page: I was the first ever to open it!

with His own infinitely compassionate nature, rather than in his perdition and therefore demands from man, as an act due from him, to turn if he would live."[43] (*emphasis mine*)

He continues: "But although He does not will, in the sense of delighting in, the death of the sinner, insofar as it means the destruction of the creature, He does not therefore cease to will and intend it as an exercise of His justice and the occasion of revealing His glory (Prov. 1:26; 1 Sam. 2:34). Even as a devout magistrate, though he does not delight in the death of criminals, yet does not cease justly to pronounce the penalty of the law."[44] (*emphasis mine*)

John Owen

By the time of John Owen, the distinction between God's revealed will and His decretive will was firmly entrenched. He saw this distinction as the embodiment of what Calvin and other divines meant when they spoke of the "one will of God" as "divers or manifold".[45] However it is doubtful that this is all that Calvin meant.

By the secret will Owen means "the unchangeable purpose concerning all things which He hath made, to be brought by certain means to their appointed ends". By the revealed will he means "our duty—not what [God] will do according to His good pleasure, but what we should do if we will please Him—this [consists] in His word, His precepts and promises".[46]

This distinction is quite legitimate. Owen however carries it to an extreme. "We must exactly distinguish between man's duty and God's purpose, there being no connection between them".[47] Owen does not give sufficient recognition to the truth that both the

43. Turretin, *Institutes of Elenctic Theology*, 4.17.33 Latin: *"ut innuatur Deum **delectari** conversionis et vita peccatoris, tanquam re sibi **grata**, et **naturae suae summe misericordi conveniente**, potius quam interitu eius, atque ideo eam exigere ab homine tanquam officium debitum, ut se convertat, si vivere cupiat."*

44. Turretin, *Elenctic Theology*, 4.17.33 Latin: *"Sed quamvis **nolit, id. non delectetur morte peccatoris**, prout notat creaturae destructionem, non desinit tamen eam velle et intendere ut exercitium iustitiae suae, et ut occasionem manifestandae gloriae, Prov 1:26, 1 Sam 2:34; ut pius Magistratus, qui **non delectatur morte reorum**, non desinit tamen eorum poenam ex Legibus iuste decernere."*

45. Owen, "Arminianism", 45.

46. Owen, "Arminianism", 45.

50. Owen, *The Death of Death*, 187.

secret will and revealed will are expressions of the same principles of God's delight. A distinction is legitimate. A dichotomy is not. Owen's theology suffers as a result.

Owen admits that God's revealed will sometimes tells us more than man's duty. Speaking of "acts" and "objects" he says that acts of God's secret will concern "what will be done" whereas His revealed will "is an act whereby he declareth Himself **to love or approve, whether ever it be done or no**". And the object of God's secret will is what is "good in any kind", whereas the object of God's revealed will is "that only which is morally good (I speak of it inasmuch as it approveth or commandeth)".[48]

For the most part however Owen maintains that the revealed will of God reveals nothing more than the duty of man. God's commands tell us nothing about God's nature, or about what God delights in. We are simply "obliged to do what He commandeth" and accept that "it is not always His pleasure that the thing itself in regard of the event shall be accomplished, as we saw before in the examples of Pharaoh and Abraham".[49] He often refers to these two examples:

God commanded Pharaoh to let His people go. According to Owen all this reveals is Pharaoh's duty; it says nothing of God's purpose.[50] The command does indeed tell us nothing about God's purpose—but it does not tell us nothing about God. For God's revealed will is a reliable witness to what God delights in. It is perfectly legitimate to assume that God delighted that Pharaoh would let the Israelites go.

Again, Owen refers to God's command to Abraham to go and sacrifice Isaac.[51] This example must be regarded as a special case of God's revealed will, and an exception is no foundation on which to build a structure of theology. If any object that I have no right to single out this example as a special case I would simply say that the linchpin of all true theology is the axiom that God's Word does not contradict itself. How then do you explain that in one part of

48. Owen, "Arminianism", 46.
49. Owen, "Arminianism", 46.
50. Owen, "Arminianism", 45; John Owen, *The Death of Death*, 200.
51. Owen, "Arminianism", 44.

Scripture God forbids child sacrifice (Deut. 12:31; Lev. 18:21, 20:1*ff*) while in this case He commands it? The only way to deal with Genesis 22 is to treat it as an exceptional case of the will of God when the Lord, for the particular purpose of testing the implicit faith of Abraham to the limit, commands him to do what His very nature abhors.

Nonetheless, so far as Abraham was concerned, he was "bound to believe" that it was not only his bare duty, but also "well pleasing unto God that he should accomplish what was enjoined", as Owen himself admits.[52] He was bound to believe that God would "love and approve this thing, whether ever it be done or no", even as he was also bound to believe that God would yet keep His promises concerning Isaac (Heb. 11:17-19). He did not try and reconcile his conflicting duties, but simply acknowledged a mystery and followed both duties in faith.

When Owen deals with the question as to whether God desires all to be saved he says much that is perceptive. We must certainly agree that Arminius' solution was intolerable. The latter proposed that God wants everyone to be saved but doesn't have the power to save them, and so is satisfied with the salvation of the few that turn of their own free will. Owen comments: "Having robbed God of His power, He will leave Him so much goodness as that He shall not be troubled at it, though He be sometimes compelled to do what He is very loath to do".[53]

Again Owen is right when he complains against those that say "there are desires in God that never are fulfilled". This leaves us with a very uncertain view of God: "Surely to desire what one is sure will never come to pass is not an act regulated by wisdom or counsel".[54] Then "God [is] in a most unhappy condition".[55]

In expounding the Ezekiel passages, however, aberrations show up in Owen's exposition—and these surely, are a result of the dichotomy he maintains between the revealed and secret will.

How does Owen deal with Ezekiel 18:23, 32 in *Death of Death*? It

52. Owen, "Arminianism", 44.
53. Owen, "Arminianism", 16.
54. Owen, "Arminianism", 25.
55. Owen, "Arminianism", 50.

should be borne in mind that he is not dealing with the "Free Offer" as such, but with Particular Atonement. Ezekiel says nothing about the atonement, so Owen's only interest in his prophecy arose from the fact that universalists appealed to it as an indirect support for universal redemption. His comments must be viewed in this light.

First, he objects that the passage does not have universal application, but should only apply to "the house of Israel".[56] But this is hardly so. God reasons with Israel on perfectly general grounds. It is because He, by His very nature, does not delight in the death of the wicked, that Israel may believe that He does not delight in the death of any particular Israelite.

Secondly, he objects that "'God willeth not the death of a sinner'" must mean either "God purposeth and determineth he shall not die", or "God commandeth that he shall do those things wherein he may live."[57] The former is out of the question, and the latter expresses nothing but God's command. But here Owen misses the whole point of the verses, which say "God has no pleasure in...", not "God willeth not...". These verses are talking about God's nature, His delight, not His will.

God expresses His command when He says *"therefore turn and live".* The word "therefore" necessarily asks the question "why should I turn and live?" And the answer is not in a bare command, nor in a decree—but in God Himself who, by His very nature, cannot take delight in the death of the sinner.

Thirdly, Owen says that the verse only has in mind temporal judgments and blessings.[58] This can hardly be so when God says He is dealing with a spiritual problem. God commands them to *"get yourselves a new heart and a new spirit"* (Ezek. 18:31). To deny that He is talking about spiritual regeneration is to deny the relevance of all similar Old Testament passages, and would lead to the view that regeneration is a blessing peculiar to the New Testament dispensation.

Fourthly, even calling the blessings and judgments temporal does not solve the problem as to how God can delight not in a

56. Owen, *The Death of Death*, 275.
57. Owen, *The Death of Death*, 275.
58. Owen, *The Death of Death*, 275.

thing and yet will it. Owen admits that the temporal judgments he ascribes to these verses were not things in themselves "so pleasurable or desirable to Him as that He did it only for His own will"—but makes no attempt to explain how God willed what He could not find "pleasurable or desirable".[59]

As one would perhaps expect, Owen is freer in his preaching than in his theologizing. In preaching on Ezekiel 33:11 and 2 Corinthians 5:20 he is able to proclaim God's "condescension that He may so entreat us that He may exercise pity, pardon, goodness, kindness, mercy towards us. He is so full, that He is, as it were, pained until He can get us to Himself, that He may communicate of His love to us.... Says God, 'O ye sons of men, why will ye die? I beseech you, be friends with Me; let us agree, accept the atonement. I have love for you; take mercy, take pardon; do not destroy your own souls... Now, 'as I live,' saith the Lord, 'I would not the death of the sinner;' Ezek. 33:11... He is of an infinite loving and tender nature; He entreats us to come to Him, and swears we shall not suffer by our so doing."[60]

Such preaching would warm the hardest heart, were it not the heart of unregenerate man. This fact Owen had in mind. He knew he could not reach the heart of the unregenerate. And so his preaching and promises were directed at those unconverted in whose hearts God was even yet working. His aim was to encourage their hearts and ours "in the belief of the promises". And therefore he freely applies the spiritual meaning of Ezekiel's plea for renewal.

It is a pity that in his theologizing he felt obliged to rationalise away the import of such passages by removing all spiritual value from them.

Other Puritan Preaching

The Puritans showed great warmth in their preaching and dwelt much on the condescension of Christ in dying for sinners. This of course is a general truth which all men should dwell upon but has specific application only for the elect. Nonetheless the Puritans also dwelt upon the nature of God which sovereignly turns to mercy and only judicially turns to judgment.

59. Owen, *The Death of Death*, 276.

60. Owen, "Arminianism", 41.

Thomas Manton writes "It suiteth more with His delight that you should take hold of these offers and not refuse them: Ezek. 33:11 'As I live, saith the Lord, I have no pleasure in the death of the wicked.' Merely as it is the destruction of the creature, so God doth not any way approve of it, though as a just punishment, He delighteth in it. If you look to God's approbation, your accepting grace more suiteth with it than your refusal."[61]

Matthew Poole comments on Ezekiel 18:23 that God is a "God of mercy, who pities, forbears and though at last hath punished obstinate sinners, yet never delighteth in their death". This verse "equally declares God's mercy and our duty, the one in His pleasure at our return, the other in our pleasing Him herein". And on Ezekiel 33:11 he says "Death is your choice, not mine.... It is your culpable will, not my severe resolution that you die".[62]

Stephen Charnock at first all but explains away any feeling in God of "joy, grief or repentance". These he explains are nothing more than anthropomorphisms,[63] since God is without passions. Joy, grief and repentance refer only to the event (i.e. such an event "that if God were capable of our passions He would discover Himself in such cases as we do"), but apparently tell us nothing about God. This incautious position could easily lead us to presume that we can never know anything about God. Despite this, Charnock deals beautifully with the attributes of God.

Charnock describes Ezekiel 33:11 as an "affectionate invitation to men", aimed, not at their destruction but their reformation.[64] God by His very nature "doth not delight in the unhappiness of any of His creatures".[65] Because of this principle in God, "punishment is not the primary intention of God". God seems to compare Himself with a good judge, who, "in the exercise of his office, doth

61. Thomas Manton, "A Practical Exposition Upon The Fifty–Third Chapter of Isaiah", *Works of Thomas Manton* (London: James Nisbet and Co., 1871), 3:330–335.
62. Matthew Poole, *Annotations upon the Holy Bible* (New York: Robert Carter and Brothers, 1853), 2:715.
63. Stephen Charnock, *The Existence and Attributes of God* (Sovereign Grace Press, 1971), 126.
64. Charnock, *The Existence and Attributes of God*, 598.
65. Charnock, *The Existence and Attributes of God*, 550.

principally intend the encouragement of the good, and wisheth[66] there were no wickedness that might occasion punishment; and when [such a judge] doth sentence a malefactor in order to the execution of him, he doth not act against the goodness of his nature, but pursuant to the duty of his place; but wisheth he had no occasion for such severity.... [God does not delight] in death as death, in punishment as punishment, but as it reduceth the suffering creature to the order of His precept or reduceth him into order under His power, or reforms others who are spectators of the punishment upon a criminal of their own nature. God only hates the sin, not the sinner. He desires only the destruction of the one, not the other."[67] The last two sentences again show a lack of caution, since, if God only wants to destroy sin, but has to destroy the sinner too, His omnipotence must be called into question, as well as the efficacy of Christ's atonement.

Patrick Fairbairn, in the 19th century, commenting on Ezekiel, expresses the compassion of God. "A yearning tenderness here manifests itself, still seeking, notwithstanding all that has taken place, the return of those who survived to the way of peace... God is anxious as a kind and affectionate parent, to see them restored to a happy, and prosperous condition." But "only if they turn from their wicked ways, can He turn from His fierce displeasure."[68]

Matthew Henry sums it up well when he says that "God's **nature, property, and delight** is to have mercy and forgive... It is true, God has determined to punish sinners, His justice calls for it, and pursuant to that, impenitent sinners will lie forever under His wrath and curse; that is the will of His decree, His consequent will, but it is not His antecedent will[69], the **will of His delight**; though the righteousness of His government requires that sinners die, yet the goodness of His nature objects against it... He is better

---

66. The words "wish", "wish not" as Charnock uses them apply to his example of a human judge, not to God Himself.
67. Charnock, *The Existence and Attributes of God*, 560.
68. Comment on Ezek. 33:11, Patrick Fairbank, *Ezekiel and the Book of His Prophecy* (Mulberry: Sovereign Grace Publishers, 1971), 360.
69. Calvinists sometimes use the terms "antecedent will" (to mean the end determined by God), and "consequent will" (to mean the means God uses to attain that end). Henry however seems to be using the terms more in an Arminian sense (see Hodge, *Systematic Theology*, 1:404.)

pleased when His mercy is glorified in their salvation, than when His justice is glorified in their damnation... The God of heaven has **no delight** in our ruin but desires our welfare".[70] (*emphasis mine*)

Both of these controversies will be discussed more fully in the third chapter. In both (especially the former), men failed to appreciate that God's "delight" concerns His nature, and not His will.

Amyraldianism and The "Marrow" Controversy

William Cunningham distinguished between God's revealed will and His decretive will and discusses the various terms used. These terms, he says, are merely a matter of usage (*usus loquendi*) employed to distinguish the "will by which God determines events" and the "will by which He determines duty".[71]

William Cunningham

Cunningham is uncertain as to just how starkly we may draw this distinction—and in this respect he retreats from the bolder position of Owen. "In the good actions of men, God's... secret and revealed will concur and combine; in their sinful actions they do not; and therefore, these latter do not express or indicate the divine will in the same sense or to the same extent, as the former".[72]

Cunningham is not averse to using the words "wish" or "desire". He maintains the law is the sort of thing God wishes or desires men to do. "Sinful actions of men are opposed to, or inconsistent with, His will as revealed in His law, which is an undoubted indication of what He wished or desired that men should do,"[73] It is evident that the law, for Cunningham, is not bare duty but expressive of the "wish" or "desire" of God. He insists that we must maintain that "in some sense God wishes as He commands and enjoins".[74]

He also believes that "all events do, as well as His law, in some sense express or indicate God's will."[75]

70. Comment on Ezek 18:23,32, Matthew Henry, *Commentary on the Whole Bible* (Peabody: Hendrickson, 1994), 1376.
71. Cunningham, *Historical Theology*, 2:454.
72. Cunningham, *Historical Theology*, 2:458.
73. Cunningham, *Historical Theology*, 2:452.
74. Cunningham, *Historical Theology*, 2:452
75. Cunningham, *Historical Theology*, 2:452.

We would assert that God's law and all events are not only indicative of His will, but expressive of His nature.

Charles Hodge

Charles Hodge also discusses the different terms used to distinguish God's will. He believes that "the decretive and preceptive will of God can never be in conflict. God never decrees [positively] to do, or to cause others to do, what He forbids".[76] God may negatively decree what He commands, but He cannot positively decree what He forbids. This is not meant to be an ultimate answer to the problem of sin.

Hodge distinguishes between "desire" and "purpose". "The English verb 'to will', sometimes expresses feeling and sometimes purpose... A judge may will the happiness of a man whom he sentences to death. He may will him not to suffer when he wills him to suffer. The infelicity of such forms of expression is that the word 'will' is used in different senses. In one part of the sentence it means desire, and in the other purpose. It is perfectly consistent therefore, that God, as a benevolent Being, should desire the happiness of all men while He purposes to save only His people."[77]

Hodge says quite plainly that God not only "delights in", but actually "desires" the salvation of all men. But he wishes to avoid any inference that God "intends" to save all men. God indeed "delights in the happiness of His creatures and when He permits them to perish, or inflicts evil upon them, it is from some inexorable necessity; that is, because it would be unwise or wrong to do otherwise".[78]

He does however recognise the difference between the will of God and the nature of God. "The will of God is the expression or revelation of His nature, or is determined by it; so that His will, as revealed, makes known to us what infinite wisdom and goodness demand."[79]

R. L. Dabney deals with the whole problem of God's desire that all

76. Hodge, *Systematic Theology*, 1:404.
77. Hodge, *Systematic Theology*, 1:405.
78. Charles Hodge, "Sermon on 1 Tim. 2:4", *Banner of Truth Magazine*, Feburary 1958.
79. Hodge, *Systematic Theology*, 1:404.

R. L. Dabney men be saved in an interesting discussion: "God's Indiscriminate Proposals of Mercy as Related to His Power, Wisdom and Sincerity".[80] He rejects any idea of universal salvation as proposed by either Arminian or Amyraldian. But he suggests that Turretin and others went too far in assuming that "as God had no volition towards the salvation of the non-elect, so He could not have any propension or affection at all towards it".

As with Turretin, Charnock, and Charles Hodge before him, Dabney uses the illustration of a just judge who condemns a criminal, whom he nonetheless feels compassion for. In Dabney's case he uses the example of George Washington, who, although he felt compassion for Major André, nonetheless condemned him to death for just reasons. André was "a major in the British Army and head of its Secret Service in America during the American Revolutionary War. He was hanged as a spy by the Continental Army for assisting Benedict Arnold's attempted surrender of the fort at West Point, New York to the British."[81]

Dabney believes Washington's decision to be basically "a complex of two elements: a desire or propension of some subjective, optative power, and a judgment of the intelligence as to the true and preferable," though "the motive of a single decision may be far more complex than this".

To the Arminian, Dabney will say that Washington's decision to put André to death does not imply impotence to save—but only that his pity was "countervailed by superior motives".

To "the other extreme" Dabney says that a decision to put André to death when it was in his power to save him does not preclude a propension to do otherwise.

With some foresight he realises that there are three main objections:

1. "Washington is not God. Washington could not meet the

---

80. R. L. Dabney, "God's Indiscriminate Proposals of Mercy", *Discussions Evangelical and Theological* (London: Banner of Truth, 1967), 1:282; For a similar discussion see R. L. Dabney, *Lectures in Systematic Theology* (Grand Rapids: Zondervan, 1972), 527–535.
81. "John André," *Wikipedia*, last modified July 29, 2020, https://en.wikipedia.org/wiki/John_Andr%C3%A9.

demands of justice. But God could, by providing atonement for the reprobate".

Dabney rightly objects that this oversimplifies the case by making impotence in God the only legitimate reason for not saving men. It would mean that God is obliged to save the elect simply because He is able to do so. It also assumes that "God's ultimate end in the government of the universe is the greatest aggregate well-being of creatures". There are many reasons, some unknown to us, why God ultimately punishes the reprobate. But no known reason denies His mercy.

2. "To speak of 'motives' behind God's actions is untenable because of:

   i. His absolute simplicity of Being.

   ii. The unity of His attributes and essence

   iii. The total lack of 'passive powers'

   iv. The unity and eternity of His will."

The first and second points are quickly dealt with. It is quite in accord with Biblical usage to distinguish motive and action, however simple the whole process may be in God. Also, although for our understanding we speak of God's attributes separately, this does not mean that we believe they are superadded to, or distinct from, His essence.

The third point is also dealt with at once. God's 'passive powers' (i.e. power, at one time, to show no affection and, at another, to show it) may be anthropopathic but "nonetheless they are affections of His will, actively distinguished from the cognitions of His intelligence". Dabney points out that God's immutability does not prevent Him showing affections such as compassion, wrath, pleasure etc. It is "active principles" in God that do not change. Because of these unchanging principles God **always** shows anger **when** men sin, **always** shows compassion **when** the creature is in trouble etc. His affections are always consistent with, and appropriate to, the occasion of their being shown. And God's affections cannot be surprised into "showing" themselves because God decrees all that comes to pass.

The fourth point objects to cause and effect within the divine will. Suffice it to say that "while the action of the divine mind in rational volition is not successive, yet its infinite capacity preserves the proper causal subordination and distinction of rational motive and resultant volition."

3. "For God to pass by a motive of compassion for a higher motive suggests unsatisfied longings in God, inward strivings and does violence to God's immutability and blessedness".

   Dabney suggests that unsatisfied longings and inward strivings arise in a man because of his passions, not because motives are complex. The saintlier a man, the less striving in following one motive and discarding another. So complex motives in God do not imply unsatisfied longings.

This is hardly a complete answer, for the more apathetic we conceive of God's longings, the more apathetic we must conceive of any compassion or desire for men in their misery.

Nonetheless, Dabney's solution is the most satisfactory answer to God's "unsatisfied longings" I have yet found. However I see no reason to posit in God a **desire** to save all when Scripture says no more than God **delights** that all would be saved.

Dabney goes on to discuss the "necessity" of God's nature of compassion, which is the source of His "free" acts of compassion—but a consideration of these matters is better left to chapter 2.

W. G. T. Shedd

As noted in the first section, W. G. T. Shedd asserts that God's "permissive decree" concerning sin is nothing more than a bare "decision", devoid of any sense of approval or pleasure. It is only God's will "in the narrow sense of volition, not in the wide sense of inclination. The will of God, in this case is only a particular decision, in order to some ulterior end. This particular decision, considered in itself, may be contrary to the abiding inclination and desire of God as founded in His holy nature."[82]

Shedd freely speaks about such a "desire" in God; he even refers to the same passage from Turretin's *Institutes* that we looked at

82. Shedd, *Dogmatic Theology*, 1:407.

before (*q.v.*) to support his view that God has a "benevolent desire" for the salvation of all men,[83] though (as we saw there) Turretin was more careful to speak of a "delight in", rather than an ambiguous "desire for". It is interesting that Shedd also quotes the case of Pharaoh. Owen said that God's command to Pharaoh indicated his duty—nothing more. Shedd says it also indicates God's desire.[84]

He proceeds on the basis of the distinction between God's revealed will and decretive will. The former is what God "is pleased with, loves, desires... and delights in". The latter is simply what He "decrees".[85] Like Cunningham he maintains that: "In the holy actions of elect men, the secret and revealed will agree. God in this case decrees what He loves. In the sinful actions of non-elect men, the two wills do not agree. God in this case decrees what He hates."[86]

Shedd also uses the word "desire" frequently in explaining Ezekiel 33:11, 18:32. What he means, though, is not God's will (as the word implies), but God's nature. "This Divine desire is constitutional. It springs from the compassionate love of the Creator towards the soul of the creature, and is founded in the essential benevolence of God."[87]

Shedd goes further than most theologians when he says "the decree of God is not always expressive of His desire, but sometimes may be contrary to it."[88] But while God is free to express or not express what is His "constitutional nature", He certainly cannot express Himself "contrary" to it. God is bound by Himself and cannot act against Himself. When He condemns the sinner to death for his sin, He may be refraining from expressing His delight that the sinner be saved, but He is not acting contrary to it. God

83. Shedd, *Dogmatic Theology*, 1:453.
84. Shedd, *Dogmatic Theology*, 1:453.
85. Shedd, *Dogmatic Theology*, 1:456.
86. Shedd, *Dogmatic Theology*, 1:456.
87. Shedd, *Dogmatic Theology*, 1:452: Some may object that a "desire" or "delight" can hardly be "constitutional" and yet "spring from" another perfection in the Divine essence. However, any expression of God's delight in Himself (which is what Shedd seems to mean) is as necessary as His nature. Any expression of God's delight outside of Himself (i.e. in His revealed will or decretive will) is free.
88. Shedd, *Dogmatic Theology*, 1:451.

cannot act against His own nature.

A. H. Strong

Augustus Hopkins Strong believes that "God's desires that certain men should be saved may not be accompanied by His will to exert special influences to save them. These desires were meant by the phrase 'revealed will' in the old theologians; His purpose to bestow special grace, by the phrase 'secret will.'"[89]

As we have seen there is some confusion as to exactly what "the old theologians" meant by God's revealed will. Men like Owen certainly did not mean desire, but most others held to some idea of a desire in God to save all.

Strong also quotes Broadus who, commenting on Matthew 6:10 "distinguishes between God's will of purpose, of desire, and of command." Such a triple distinction is unwarranted and clarifies nothing. It would not be unfair to label Strong as Amyraldian.[90]

Louis Berkhof

Louis Berkhof discusses the various terms used to distinguish the will of God and points out that the pairs of terms used in Reformed theology do not always draw exactly the same distinction—but each highlights some particular truth.[91] He adds that "the decretive and preceptive will of God do not conflict in the sense that in the former He does, and according to the latter He does not, take pleasure in sin; nor in the sense that according to the former He does not, and according to the latter He does, will the salvation of every individual with a positive volition. Even according to the decretive will God takes no pleasure in sin; and even according to the preceptive will He does not will the salvation of every individual with a positive volition."[92] On God's decree to permit sin he states that "while it renders the entrance of sin into the world certain, it does not mean that God takes delight in it; but only that He deemed it wise for the purpose of His self-revelation, to permit moral evil, however abhorrent it may be to His nature."[93]

---

89. Augustus H. Strong, *Systematic Theology* (Old Tappan: Fleming H. Revell, 1976), 791.
90. Strong, *Systematic Theology*, 771–773.
91. Berkhof, *Systematic Theology*, 77.
92. Berkhof, *Systematic Theology*, 79.
93. Berkhof, *Systematic Theology*, 108..

Like most consistent Reformed theologians Berkhof concedes that, for our understanding, we must conceive of God as taking counsel "before" He actually decreed, and His decree is thereby based upon a weighing up of all contingent considerations.[94] Not all these considerations are known to man and it would therefore be highly presumptuous of man to pontificate as to how God should act.

Berkhof regards both the decretive will and revealed will as manifestations of the nature of God. His law not only tells man his duty, but also manifests God's holiness.[95] And His decree is an "internal manifestation and exercise of the divine essence."[96]

Murray, Stonehouse and the Orthodox Presbyterian Church

The purpose of John Murray and Ned Stonehouse's booklet *"The Free Offer of the Gospel"* is to prove that it can properly be said that "God **desires** the salvation of all men".[97]

As mentioned earlier, Murray and Stonehouse note that "desire" is "not necessarily the most accurate and felicitous word," but claim that they use it because it "has come to be used in the debate".[98] There is little doubt about this.

They would, of course, be better off using the word "delight". Their use of the word "desire" is the source of a multitude of troubles. One is never certain when they are talking about God's nature and when about God's will. They say, for instance, that "in predicating such 'desire' of God, [the Committee of the O.P.C.] was not dealing with the decretive will of God, ... but the revealed will".[99] But later on they say that what is expressed is "not simply the bare preceptive will of God but the disposition of loving kindness on the part of God".[100]

Murray and Stonehouse give a useful exposition of Ezekiel and show that the meaning is not that "God delights **when** the wicked

---

94. Berkhof, *Systematic Theology*, 101f.
95. Berkhof, *Systematic Theology*, 74.
96. Berkhof, *Systematic Theology*, 103.
97. Murray and Stonehouse, *The Free Offer of the Gospel*, 3.
98. Murray and Stonehouse, *The Free Offer of the Gospel*, 4.
99. Murray and Stonehouse, *The Free Offer of the Gospel*, 3.
100. Murray and Stonehouse, *The Free Offer of the Gospel*, 4.

turn" but "God delights **that** the wicked turn". "When the object is contemplated as desirable, but not actually realised, the thought of *chaphez* [chaphets] does not at all appear to be simply that delight or pleasure will be derived from the object **when** it is realised or possessed. That thought is of course implied. But there is much more. There is the delight or pleasure or desire **that** it should come to be even if the actual occurrence should never take place".[101]

They reconcile this with God's decree of reprobation by saying: "We are not here speaking of God's decretive will. In terms of His decretive will it must be said that God absolutely decrees the eternal death of some wicked, and in that sense is absolutely pleased so to decree. But in the text it is the will of God's benevolence (*voluntas euarestias*) that is stated, not the will of God's decree (*voluntas eudokias*)."[102]

Once again this is far from clear. God cannot be pleased according to His secret will and not pleased according to His revealed will. This is to make God (in Calvin's words) "two faced".[103] To say God is "pleased" implies something about His nature, not His will. He cannot be two things in His nature at the same time.

If we speak of God's "good pleasure" to refer to His decree we do not necessarily mean that God is pleased with, in the sense that He delights in, the event decreed. As we showed at the beginning of this chapter God's "good pleasure" (in that sense) may refer to His bare will. Any pleasure in the decree of punishment is not in the misery of the creature, but in seeing His justice and righteousness vindicated.

Like Calvin, Murray and Stonehouse maintain that God may "earnestly desire the fulfilment of something which He has not, in the exercise of His sovereign will actually decreed to come to pass".[104] "This is indeed mysterious, and why He has not brought to pass, in the exercise of His omnipotent power and grace, what is His ardent pleasure lies hid in the sovereign counsel of His will. We

---

101. Murray and Stonehouse, *The Free Offer of the Gospel*, 17.
102. Murray and Stonehouse, *The Free Offer of the Gospel*, 19.
103. I am not certain that Calvin can be absolved from the same charge, even though he insists God's will is "twofold", not "two faced".
104. Murray and Stonehouse, *The Free Offer of the Gospel*, 10.

should not entertain, however, any prejudice against the notion that God desires, or has pleasure in, the accomplishment of what He does not decretively will".[105] We would do well to heed Murray and Stonehouse's warning and realise that simple "logic" is not sufficient evidence to destroy the notion that God can decree what He has no pleasure in.

However Murray and Stonehouse fail to the last to distinguish between God's nature and His will. They conclude by saying, "The loving and benevolent will that is the source of that offer and that grounds its veracity and reality is the will to the possession of Christ and the enjoyment of the salvation that resides in him."[106]

What do they mean? How does God "will" that the reprobate will possess Christ? Only by confusing "pleasure, will, desire" are they able to postulate that the reprobate are the subjects of "the loving and benevolent will to the possession of Christ".

Murray and Stonehouse could have done much more to keep the issues clear.

R. B. Kuiper

R. B. Kuiper espouses the position that "God will be pleased to save [sinners everywhere] if they repent and believe. Yet that is not all. They are to be told that the God of infinite love will be pleased to see them repent, believe and be saved."[107] This is quite scriptural though one might well ask why he connects God's infinite love and the free offer. Is he trying to blur the distinction between God's redemptive love for His elect and general love for mankind?

He then goes further to say that God "desires the salvation of every sinner reached by the gospel".[108] Even in this he has only reiterated what many another theologian has already said.

But when he says that: "John 3:16 and Romans 5:6,8 were not written for the elect alone", but tell of "a universal love of God"[109] he is on dangerous ground indeed. If he means that the truths of

105. Murray and Stonehouse, *The Free Offer of the Gospel*, 26.
106. Murray and Stonehouse, *The Free Offer of the Gospel*, 27.
107. R. B. Kuiper, *God Centred Evangelism* (London: Banner of Truth, 1966), 31.
108. Kuiper, *God Centred Evangelism*, 31.
109. R. B. Kuiper, *The Glorious Body of Christ* (London: Banner of Truth, 1967), 180.

John 3 and Romans 5 are to be preached to all then he is certainly right. But if he means that God loves all men with that intense and special love described in John 3 and Romans 5 then he can only spread a false sense of security amongst hearers of the Word who will "trust" in God's general benevolence rather than come to Him through faith and repentance. It is by no means clear what his exact meaning is when he says these verses "were not written for the elect alone".

In commenting on Ezekiel he asserts God's desire to save all and insists that such preaching is not to be neglected in presenting the gospel.[110]

Erroll Hulse

Erroll Hulse follows in the wake of Murray and Stonehouse and adds little to what has already been said. He maintains that God "desires" and "wishes" the salvation of all,[111] but avoids much of the ambiguity of the Murray and Stonehouse reasoning.

Concerning a distinction in the will of God, Hulse will only assert that "the Scriptures indicate that we are obliged to distinguish carefully between God's revealed will and His decretive or secret will (Deut. 29:29)."[112] If we ask "If God desires, yes, wills all men to be saved, why are they not saved?" we can only answer "Why should God do anything benevolent for those who curse Him? He is not obligated".[113]

Protestant Reformed Church

As mentioned previously (p. 8), the Protestant Reformed Church bases its reasoning on the following "logic":

- The reprobate is the object of God's hatred.
- Because of God's hatred the reprobate is doomed.
- How can it be said that God desires the salvation of the reprobate?[114]

---

110. R.B. Kuiper, *The Bible Tells Us So* (London: Banner of Truth, 1968), 66; Kuiper, *The Glorious Body of Christ*, 174, 231.
111. Erroll Hulse, *The Free Offer* (Haywards Heath: Carey Publication, 1973), 7.
112. Hulse, *The Free Offer*, 8.
113. Hulse, *The Free Offer*, 9.
114. Homer C. Hoeksema, "The O.P.C. and the 'Free Offer'" *Standard Bearer*, 15th September 1973, 1st January 1974; David Engelsma, "'Hyper-Calvinism' and the Call of the Gospel" *Standard Bearer*, 1st April 1974.

We have already shown that the word "desire" is pregnant with ambiguity. However, to say that "God would delight in the salvation of the reprobate" is no solution for them either.[115]

We must reject this kind of rationalisation. Heretics from Arius to Arminius have erred by following through a few simple syllogisms and although the above is not the only foundation of Protestant Reformed Church theology, it is nonetheless the constant court of appeal in their "free offer" reasoning. I will deal with God's "hate of the reprobate" in the next chapter, but I mention this "logic" of theirs now because it is the linchpin of their arguments.

Rationalising assumes great importance in their arguing. "We must bear in mind that Scripture is 'rational,'[116] that is understandable. In Holy Scripture God reveals Himself to us exactly in such a way that our 'finite minds' may be able to grasp that revelation as one, harmonious whole".[117]

Poor Calvin! Although he admitted that Scripture was harmonious he confessed that he could not always grasp how. "Since, on account of the dullness of our sense, the wisdom of God seems manifold (or, as an old interpreter rendered it, multiform) are we, therefore, to dream of some variation in God, as if He either changed His counsel, or disagreed with Himself? Nay, when we cannot comprehend how God can will that to be done which He forbids us to do, let us call to mind our imbecility, and remember that the light in which He dwells is not, without cause, termed inaccessible (1 Tim. 6:6), because shrouded in darkness."[118]

Understandably the Protestant Reformed Church objects to Murray and Stonehouse—and some of their objections are well founded. H. C. Hoeksema says that Murray and Stonehouse present a "two faced" (*my word, not theirs*) God. There is a "contradiction and conflict between God's being and God's revelation... A doctrine of two wills in God is a denial of [God's]

115. H. C. Hoeksema, "O.P.C. and the 'Free Offer'", 1st November 1973.

116. I am not suggesting that to call the scripture "rational" is rationalising. Rationalising arises from imagining you can "grasp" the entire "harmony" of Scripture, despite your "dullness' and "imbecility".

117. Homer C. Hoeksema, "Question Box" *Standard Bearer* 1st May 1973, 1st June 1974.

118. Calvin, *Institutes*, 1.18.3.

attributes [of unity and simplicity]".[119]

H. C. Hoeksema also takes on Murray and Stonehouse for their use of loose terminology when they talk of a will that is "not God's decretive will," but neither is it "the bare preceptive will".[120]

Hoeksema does tend to split hairs though in his criticism. He objects that Murray and Stonehouse are pulling a sleight-of-hand when they assume the invitation of the gospel is at least the bare preceptive will of God.[121] He also objects to them stating that repentance and faith are "conditions" attached to the gospel offer, saying this lands them "squarely in the Arminian camp"![122] How meticulously and cautiously such a man must tread in case the word "if" ever falls from his lips between a preaching on salvation and then a preaching on repentance and faith![123]

Despite Hoeksema's complaint against Murray and Stonehouse, he himself never comes to grips with what he means by the "will" of God. By another piece of "logic" he reasons:

- "God wills the damnation of the reprobate [i.e. secret will].
- "God wills the salvation of the reprobate [i.e. revealed will].
- "No amount of mental gymnastics can persuade one to accept both".[124]

Now in so far as Murray and Stonehouse confuse God's nature and His will, Hoeksema is right. But as two propositions stating God's revealed will and His secret will they are easily reconciled if one refers to God's command and the other to God's purpose. In fact, every reputable Reformed theologian up until this day has

---

119. H. C. Hoeksema, "O.P.C. and the 'Free Offer', 1st May 1973.
120. H. C. Hoeksema, "O.P.C. and the 'Free Offer', 15th September 1973, 1st November 1973.
121. H. C. Hoeksema, "O.P.C. and the 'Free Offer', 1st November 1973.
122. H. C. Hoeksema, "O.P.C. and the 'Free Offer', 15th December 1973.
123. The Westminster Divines used the word "condition" (WLC. 32; The Sum of Saving Knowledge 3; The Practical Use of Saving Knowledge 4) and we should not be afraid of it. We must, of course guard against any Arminian connotation. Turretin spoke of an "instrumental cause", not a "meritorious cause" (quoted by Thomas *q.v.*). Bavinck said there were conditions "in the covenant" not "to the covenant" (Berkhof, *Systematic Theology*, 277, also 281). Pierre Marcel also speaks of conditions "in the covenant" not "of the covenant". Pierre Marcel, *The Biblical Doctrine of Infant Baptism* (London: James Clarke, 1953), 102.
124. H. C. Hoeksema, "O.P.C. and the 'Free Offer', 1st May 1973.

been able to understand what is meant.

As pointed out earlier Engelsma and Hoeksema differ as to the correct interpretation of Article 8, Heads 3 and 4, Canons of Dort. One explains it away by saying it is the "activity" of coming that is "pleasing", and the other says that the "hearers" themselves are in mind, but their coming (which never eventuates) is only "right", not "pleasing". Thus, in one way or another the passage in Ezekiel is explained away.

Hoeksema protests that to say "God delights that those to whom the offer comes would enjoy what is offered in its fullness" is nothing but Arminianism and contradicts the Reformed position.[125] One is compelled to ask "Which Reformed position?" Certainly not the one in which most since Calvin's day have stood. To say that these doctrines have been "developed by the Christian Reformed Church and by the Orthodox Presbyterian Church"[126] is just not true. It is to ignore the history of theology.

Evangelical Presbyterian Church

The Evangelical Presbyterian Church in Australia takes a similar position to the Protestant Reformed Church on whether God "desires the salvation of all men". Charles Rodman, however, is not averse to saying that God "wills all to be saved" as long as, by that "will", is meant God's precept.[127] Evidently he is a more agile mental gymnast than Hoeksema.

The Evangelical Presbyterian Church is quite right when it says "It would be contrary to Scripture and to reason to suppose that there is a desire in God which is without sensibility and reason, and which does not belong to His internal mind."[128] A desire cannot be sensibly posited in an external precept.

Rodman strikes at the root of the matter when he says that "God

125. H. C. Hoeksema, "O.P.C. and the 'Free Offer'", 1st November 1973.
126. Engelsma, "'Hyper-Calvinism' and the Call of the Gospel", 1st April 1974.
127. Charles Rodman, "*The Desire of God for the Salvation of the Reprobate" An ambiguous doctrine refuted and the Reformed Evangelical Church vindicated* (EPCA, n.d.), 2.
128. Charles Rodman, *Universalism and the Reformed Churches: A Defence of Calvin's Calvinism* (EPCA, n.d.), 16.

gives grace and repentance according to His desire and purpose".[129] This immediately brings to the fore the volitional aspect of "desire" and its unsuitableness in the present debate. For how can God desire the salvation of the reprobate without desiring their repentance? Murray and Stonehouse gloss over the issue by simply stating that "it amounts to the same thing to say "God desires their salvation" as to say "He desires their repentance"."[130] This however does not overcome the difficulty. Traditionally Reformed theology has tried to side step the issue by saying that God desires their salvation, but the barrier (which He chooses not to overcome) has been lack of repentance. But to say that God also "desires" their repentance should remove all barriers between God's desire and the fulfilment of that desire.

The above objections do not apply if we say "God delights that all men would repent and be saved". This is a purely constitutional aspect of God's nature, and says nothing about the free expression of such in His will.

It is doubtful however that Rodman would accept even this statement. He hinges his theology on Owen's dichotomy: "there is no connection between man's duty and God's purpose". Like Owen he quotes the example of Abraham being commanded to offer up Isaac and asks if we are to believe that God desired to see Isaac slain.[131] We have already noted that it is a weak structure of theology that bases itself upon what must be regarded as an exception to the rule. In any case Abraham's faith is hardly a good basis for Rodman's rationalistic theology. For Abraham believed that God would raise up the promised seed through Isaac even if he were sacrificed. Let Rodman rationalise faith like that the same way he does God's command. Even Owen accepted that Abraham was "bound to believe that it was well pleasing to God" and that He "loved and approved this thing". We are bound to believe that the revealed will commands what God delights in.

For Rodman, reprobation is nothing more than a means to an end—the provision of a pool of wicked men required to

129. Rodman, "*The Desire of God for the Salvation of the Reprobate*", 2.

130. Murray and Stonehouse, *The Free Offer of the Gospel*, 4.

131. Rodman, "*The Desire of God for the Salvation of the Reprobate*", 2.

accomplish God's purposes for the elect. "If God had not purposed that wicked men by His determinate counsel should take and slay the Lord Jesus, how then would He have accomplished His desire in the salvation of His people?".[132] This is an amazing statement. If I had been there would not I have gone along with the crowd that crucified my Lord, and Rodman too—not to mention 3000 others (Acts 2:36) from the elect who would later on have been saved (Acts 2:41). Since when have the reprobate alone indulged in wickedness?

Rodman sees an unfulfilled desire in God as an imperfection of His nature. Such a proposition is a "very serious weakness" in the Murray and Stonehouse doctrine.[133] He also quotes Calvin where he speaks of what appears to be "great variety" in God's will because of our own weakness. But he adds that for Calvin "the simplicity of will and singleness of purpose of God is axiomatic in his theology".[134]

It is axiomatic in all reputable theologies. The question is not whether God's purpose is single but how we are to understand the apparent variety of purpose. How can we best conceive of the nature of God despite our own weakness? Calvin, Cunningham, Hodge and Dabney all concede that there is a mystery.

Hoeksema and Rodman see no mystery.

3. The Testimony of Scripture

As well as those Scriptures already considered, we could consider the following:

Deut. 5:29 *"Oh, that they had such a heart in them that they would fear Me and always keep all My commandments, that it might be well with them and with their children forever!"*

Deut. 32:29 *"Oh, that they were wise, that they understood this, that they would consider their latter end!"*

Psa. 81:13 *"Oh, that My people would listen to Me, that Israel*

132. Rodman, "*The Desire of God for the Salvation of the Reprobate*", 3.
133. Rodman, "*The Desire of God for the Salvation of the Reprobate*", 5.
134. Rodman, "*The Desire of God for the Salvation of the Reprobate*", 6.

would walk in My ways!"

Isa. 48:18 *"Oh, that you had heeded My commandments!"*

These verses are a consistent expression of God's delight that men would turn to Him. To imagine that these verses embrace only the elect is entirely unwarranted. Even if they did, it does not explain how God can express His nature as delighting in what never occurred (as in *"Oh that they had..."* etc).

Some explain this by saying that *"O that..."* should be translated *"if"*. Such a construction, to make sense, would require an apodosis which is non-existent in Deuteronomy 32:29. Murray and Stonehouse point out that there can be no doubt about the optative force of these four verses expressing a "strong desire".[135]

Owen explains away any heart in these verses in much the same way as he dealt with Ezekiel. The answers to his objections are the same. He also says "that desires and wishings should properly be ascribed unto God is exceedingly opposite to His all-sufficiency and the perfection of His nature".[136] He explains that such are anthropomorphisms—but fails to demonstrate in what way they are. Finally he says that God only expresses Himself this way so as to draw us to Himself. Matthew Poole makes a similar statement.[137]

Charnock, however, sees Psalm 81:13 as more than just an earnest invitation. He exclaims "how meltingly doth He bewail man's wilful refusal of His goodness".[138]

Matthew Henry also sees, not just an invitation, but an expression of God's nature. "The God of heaven is truly and earnestly desirous of the welfare and salvation of poor sinners.... He delights not in the ruin of sinful persons or nations."[139]

Dabney asserts that "God seems to express a yearning compassion for sinners," but it is "entirely consistent for God to compassionate where He never purposed nor promised to save, because this sincere compassion was restrained within the limits

135. Murray and Stonehouse, *The Free Offer of the Gospel*, 9.
136. Owen, *The Death of Death*, 289.
137. Poole, *Annotations*, 1:401.
138. Charnock, *The Existence and Attributes of God*, 599.
139. Matthew Henry, *Commentary on the Whole Bible* (Peabody: Hendrickson, 1994), 243.

God announced by His own wisdom."[140]

Lam. 3:33 *"He does not afflict willingly* (Heb *leb* i.e. from the heart) *nor grieve the children of men".*

This verse expresses the fact that God does not always delight in the event itself even though it be His decree.

Both Charnock[141] and Poole[142] refer to Isaiah 28:21 saying judgment is God's "strange work": "Mercy is His proper natural work, which floweth from Himself without any cause in the creature. Judgment is His strange work to which He never proceedeth but when provoked, and, as it were forced from the creature, whence it followeth that He cannot delight in it." Matthew Henry[143] and Charles Hodge[144] write in a similar vein.

Hos. 11:8 *"How can I give you up, Ephraim? How can I hand you over, Israel? ...My heart churns within Me; My sympathy is stirred."*

This verse refers specifically to Israel, but not only to the elect in Israel. According to Matthew Poole the verse suggests a debate between God's justice and mercy—though this must be understood anthropomorphically.[145] Calvin agrees and adds that the verse also teaches that God "is not carried away too suddenly to inflict punishment, even when men in various ways provoke His vengeance".[146] Matthew Henry expresses the same sentiment by: "The God of heaven is slow to anger and is especially loth to abandon a people to utter ruin, that has been in special relation to Him."[147]

---

140. Dabney, "God's Indiscriminate Proposals of Mercy", 307*f.*
141. Charnock, *The Existence and Attributes of God*, 560.
142. Poole, *Annotations*, 2:390.
143. Henry, *Commentary*, 1330.
144. Hodge, *"Sermon on 1 Tim. 2:4"*, 17.
145. Poole, *Annotations*, 2:878.
146. John Calvin, *Commentaries on the Minor Prophets* (Edinburgh: Calvin Translation Society, 1846), 1:401.
147. Henry, *Commentary*, 1487.

Luke 19:41*f* *"Now as He drew near, He saw the city and wept over it, saying, 'If you had known, even you, especially in this your day, the things that make for your peace! But now they are hidden from your eyes.'"*

Matt. 23:37 *"O Jerusalem, Jerusalem, the one who kills the prophets and stones those who are sent to her! How often I wanted to gather your children together, as a hen gathers her chicks under her wings, but you were not willing!"*

It should be noted that these verses refer to two separate occasions, and although often quoted together, the former speaks more of the compassion of Christ, the latter of His indignation.[148] Both express His grief.[149]

Both Calvin[150] and Owen[151] understand the expression of Christ's feeling to be anthropopathic. In this of course they mean a whole lot more than what that term usually implies—because Christ was not just God expressing His feelings in terms understandable to humans: He was human Himself. Perhaps this explains what Charnock meant when he said "that if God were capable of our passions He would discover Himself in such cases as we do". Christ is the ultimate Anthropomorphism. What we conceive of as delight in God, expresses itself as a desire when God becomes man.

Calvin also comments that it is in His special office as Mediator that Christ weeps. He came as a Saviour, "the man Christ Jesus" and as such "wished that His coming might bring salvation to all". It is frivolous to say that Christ only desired these things because He was ignorant of who was elect or reprobate (He was, after all, lamenting over a city already lost), or that He bewailed these things because He was powerless to act. Nonetheless some have suggested that Christ here expresses human feelings and desires and as such we learn nothing of the nature of God.

148. John Calvin, *Commentary on a Harmony of the Evangelists Matthew, Mark, and Luke* (Edinburgh: Calvin Translation Society, 1846), 3:105–106.

149. Manton, "A Practical Exposition", 330–335.

150. Calvin, *Commentary on a Harmony of the Evangelists Matthew, Mark, and Luke*, 3:105–106.

151. Owen, *The Death of Death*, 288.

First we acknowledge that if it were any other human this argument might carry some weight. But we are talking about Humanity in its perfect state. Are we to believe that "holy humanity is more generous and tender than God" (Dabney)[152] The Evangelical Presbyterian Church would say yes.[153]

Secondly both Dabney as well as Murray and Stonehouse[154] point out that the fact that Christ is speaking here as Messiah means He is speaking as God-man. We are not talking about feelings peculiar to human nature such as hunger or tiredness. Christ is speaking of "gathering" and "saving". He speaks as a Saviour and Mediator. Calvin therefore admits "that here Christ speaks not only in the character of man".[155]

Nor should we blasphemously suggest that weeping was unbecoming to Christ's perfection. "Those who think that it was idle for Him to weep for that which He might easily have helped, seem to oblige God to give out of His grace, whether men do what He hath commanded them, and is in their power to do, yea or no".[156]

Matthew 23:37 and Luke 19:41 can only be viewed as an expression of the divine nature through human forms; such an expression being the supreme example of anthropomorphism.

Therefore Shedd[157], Charnock[158], Hodge[159] and Henry[160] have no hesitation in saying that "with tears and sighs He bewails the ruin of Jerusalem. He desires not their ruin. He delights in their repentance". Berkhof also refers to this passage as evidence of God's "favourable disposition".[161]

H. C. Hoeksema climbs out on a limb with John Gill. He interprets this passage as "O Jerusalem (the city)—how often would I have

152. Dabney, "God's Indiscriminate Proposals of Mercy", 308.
153. Rodman, *Universalism and the Reformed Churches*, 11–12.
154. Murray and Stonehouse, *The Free Offer of the Gospel*, 12.
155. Calvin, *Institutes*, 3.24.17.
156. Poole, *Annotations*, 3:261–262.
157. Shedd, *Dogmatic Theology*, 1:453.
158. Charnock, *The Existence and Attributes of God,* 599.
159. Hodge, *"Sermon on 1 Tim. 2:4"*, 17.
160. Henry, *Commentary*, 1737.
161. Berkhof, *Systematic Theology*, 446.

gathered thy children (the elect of the city) together, but ye (the city) would not (allow Me to do so)",[162] *cf* Gill quoted by G. H. Clark.[163] Such an interpretation strains exegesis somewhat.

---

1 Tim. 2:4 *"God will have all men to be saved and to come unto the knowledge of the truth".*

The context is especially important here. Paul was writing to Timothy in a day of ungodly leaders—kings and other authorities who persecuted the church. Some Christians apparently felt they should not pray for such. Paul says they should not feel that way and states the reason in 1 Timothy 2:4.

Now it would seem that Paul's advice assumes that "prayer is an offering up of our desires unto God, for things agreeable to His will".[164]. By this we mean God's revealed will, which reveals not only God's command but also God's nature. We should therefore feel free to pray for anyone since it is agreeable to God that all men would turn to Him, as is evident from His universal command.

This is the view of Poole,[165] and Manton.[166] Charles Hodge goes further and says this verse teaches "God desires the salvation of all".[167] Matthew Henry[168] agrees, while Berkhof uses the verse also to show that God has a universal "favourable disposition".[169]

Another interpretation is sometimes given which may be more acceptable. This says that we should not feel restrained in praying for a particular "king" or "authority" simply because we believe that God may have written off this type of person. Amongst God's elect are rich and poor, fools and wise, male and female—no class is to be written off. Hendriksen[170] defends this view, as does

---

162. H. C. Hoeksema, "Question Box".
163. G. H. Clark, *Biblical Predestination* (Philadelphia: P&R 1969), 136.
164. WSC Q.98.
165. Poole, *Annotations*, 3:777.
166. Manton, "A Practical Exposition", 330–335.
167. Hodge, *"Sermon on 1 Tim. 2:4"*, 17.
168. Henry, *Commentary*, 2352.
169. Berkhof, *Systematic Theology*, 446.
170. William Hendriksen, *A Commentary on I Timothy* (London: Banner of Truth, 1964), 96.

Herman Hoeksema,[171] Calvin[172] and Owen.[173] Owen, in particular, objects to the former view on the ground that we ought not to pray for every man (1 John 5:16; John 17:9)—but those texts do not prevent prayer for a sinner in general: John in his epistle will not encourage prayer in a particular case (apostasy), and Christ was simply praying specifically for His disciples at the time. On the other hand the example of Paul (Rom. 9:1–3, 10:1) shows that, in prayer, "the settled boundary of love is, that it proceeds as far as conscience permits".[174]

Other verses will be considered in the following chapters.

171. H. C. Hoeksema, "The O.P.C. and the 'Free Offer'", 15th May 1973.
172. Calvin, *Institutes*, 3.24.16; Calvin, *Eternal Predestination*, 105,149; John Calvin, *Commentaries on the Epistles to Timothy, Titus, and Philemon* (Edinburgh: Calvin Translation Society, 1856), 54–55.
173. Owen, *The Death of Death*, 197, 231, 269, 275, 281.
174. John Calvin, *Commentary on the Epistle of Paul the Apostle to the Romans* (Edinburgh: Calvin Translation Society, 1849), 54–55 *cf* Canons of Dort 3 & 4.15.

Chapter Two

GOD'S GOODNESS TO MEN IN GENERAL

We come now to the second question arising from Engelsma's summing up: Does God offer the gospel to all because He loves all? Does He love all?

This question has invariably been linked with that of "Common Grace" and we begin with an examination of the development of that doctrine.

1. The Development of the Traditional Doctrine of "Common Grace" up to 1924

John Calvin

There is no doubt that Calvin held to a view of common grace, by which he meant a favour in God towards men in general whereby He gives them various gifts. "This is a grace which is communal, does not pardon nor purify human nature, and does not affect the salvation of sinners".[1]

Such grace restrains sin. Calvin states: "We ought to consider that, notwithstanding of the corruption of our nature, there is some room for divine grace, such grace as, without purifying it, may lay it under internal restraint".[2] In the elect God cures their sin, but in others He only lays their sin under restraint. If He did not, He could not preserve "the established order of things".[3] Calvin goes as far as to say that the reprobate sometimes partakes of a form of special grace, which God later withdraws on account of his ingratitude.[4]

But there is a second aspect of common grace. By it men's efforts, especially with regard to "inferior objects", are not fruitless;

1. Berkhof, *Systematic Theology*, 434.
2. Calvin, *Institutes*, 2.3.3.
3. Calvin, *Institutes*, 2.3.3.
4. Calvin, *Institutes*, 3.24.8.

and "even with regard to superior objects... he makes some little progress".[5] Calvin recalls the (secular) "writings of the ancients" and exclaims "shall we deem anything to be noble and praiseworthy, without tracing it to the hand of God?"[6] He speaks of "the general kindness of God" and the "Divine indulgence" whereby we retain the "property of reason" within our nature. We ought therefore to avail ourselves of the fruit of such reasoning in "physics, dialectics, mathematics and other similar sciences".[7] All these are gifts of the "Divine Spirit" who "dispenses to whom He will for the common benefit of mankind".[8]

It should be noted that by common grace Calvin does not mean a grace given to all men equally. "Some excel in acuteness, and some in judgment, while others have greater readiness in learning some peculiar act, [and] God, by this variety, commends His favour toward us, lest anyone should presume to arrogate to himself that which flows from His mere liberality. For whence is it that one is more excellent than another but that in a common nature the grace of God is especially displayed in passing by many, and thus proclaiming that it is under obligation to none".[9] Calvin therefore sometimes calls common grace "special",[10] by which he means that even in dispensing gifts of the Spirit to men in general God is particular. However while all such gifts are God's "kindness to the human race",[11] they are defiled by unregenerate men in whom "there is no zeal for the glory of God".[12]

From Calvin to Hodge

"Since the days of Calvin the doctrine of common grace was generally recognised in Reformed theology, though it also met with occasional opposition. For a long time however, little was done to develop the doctrine. This was in all probability due to the fact that the rise and prevalence of rationalism made it necessary to place all emphasis

5. Calvin, *Institutes*, 2.2.13.
6. Calvin, *Institutes*, 2.2.15.
7. Calvin, *Institutes*, 2.2.15f.
8. Calvin, *Institutes*, 2.215f.
9. Calvin, *Institutes*, 2.2.17.
10. Calvin, *Institutes*, 2.2.14; 2.3.4.
11. Calvin, *Institutes*, 2.3.4.
12. Calvin, *Institutes*, 2.3.4.

on special grace".[13]

The Synod of Dort simply acknowledged in passing that "there remain in man since the fall, the glimmerings of natural light, whereby he retains some knowledge of God, of natural things, and of the difference between good and evil, and shows some regard for virtue and good behaviour". Such light of nature is unable to lead a man to salvation and is polluted and corrupted by sinful man.[14]

The Westminster Confession does not deal with common grace though it does admit that the non-elect "may have common operations of the Spirit".[15]

Owen only barely touches upon common grace, by which he means a specific influence of the Spirit in those that hear the gospel. "Common or general grace consisteth in the external revelation of the will of God by His word, with some illumination of the mind to perceive it, and correction of the affections not too much to contemn it; and this, in some degree or other, to some more, to some less, is common to all that are called".[16] Shedd quotes a similar passage from Owen's *Dominion of Sin and Grace* (Works VII), but it is doubtful that this is actually talking about common grace and not simply the offer of special grace.[17]

Although Owen sees grace as a specific work of the Spirit, he also speaks of a "general compassion in God, by which He proceeds in the dispensation of His providence";[18] but he warns that men may not thereby rest secure thinking God will not judge them, for God's natural compassion towards men ceased with the fall and any pity He now shows is by an act of sovereign will.[19] The sinner in his misery ought not therefore presume upon the goodness of God, since any compassion God shows is not because his state deserves it, but because God, in His grace, chooses to show it. It is

13. Berkhof, *Systematic Theology*, 434.
14. Canons of Dort 3 & 4.4.
15. WCF 10.4.
16. Owen, "Arminianism", 134.
17. Shedd, *Dogmatic Theology*, 3:423.
18. John Owen, "The Strength of Faith", *Works of John Owen* (London: Banner of Truth, 1968), 10:39.
19. Owen, "The Strength of Faith", 39.

by grace God shows compassion to the sinner, and not because of compassion alone. Thus Owen does not rule out the goodness of God to men generally. He simply removes any obligation on God's part to show it to those who have forfeited it.

Other puritan preaching often embraced the doctrine of the goodness of God. Many of their works call sinners to come to Christ and display the kindness of God to even fallen creation to show that God is not an implacable, malevolent deity—but is rather ready to receive and bless them. They also "dwelt on the patience and forbearance expressed in [God's] invitations to sinners as further revealing His kindness".[20] It was this concept of the goodness of God that was stressed, rather than the theological term "common grace".

Charnock expresses the goodness of God as "His inclination to deal well and bountifully with His creatures".[21] It needs to be reaffirmed though, that while God has this inclination, He does not automatically manifest it to those who have forfeited it, but only by His grace.

Charles Hodge

Hodge expounds the doctrine of "common grace" systematically. By such he does not mean God's compassionate dealings in providence but a specific "work" or "influence of the Spirit of God on the minds of men".[22] "The Holy Spirit... is present with every human mind, enforcing truth, restraining from evil, exciting to good, and imparting wisdom or strength, when, where, and in what measure seemeth to Him good".[23] This influence is evidenced in God's striving with men (Gen. 6:3). Such an influence may be resisted (Acts 7:51), grieved, vexed or quenched. As God's severest judgment the Spirit may be withdrawn (Rom. 1:25–28; Psa. 81:11–12). The apparent conversion of the unregenerate is also the work of the Spirit (Heb. 6:4).[24]

Common grace is important in preserving order in society which is thereby kept from degenerating into a state of hell. The influence

20. J.I. Packer, *Evangelism and the Sovereignty of God* (London: IVF 1967), 18.
21. Charnock, *The Existence and Attributes of God*, 541.
22. Hodge, *Systematic Theology*, 2:655,665.
23. Hodge, *Systematic Theology*, 2:667.
24. Hodge, *Systematic Theology*, 2:668*f.*

of the Spirit is responsible for "all the decorum, order, refinement, and virtue existing among men"; for a "general fear of God" in society; and (as already mentioned) for the apparent conversion of the unregenerate.[25]

All these operations of the Spirit "in a greater or less degree are common to all men".[26]

W. G. T. Shedd

Shedd also distinguishes between "special or regenerating grace" and "common grace". The latter is not excluded in the decree of reprobation.[27] The texts he quotes as evidence are the same as those quoted by Hodge.

All men receive some grace. "The impenitent shall not be condemned for want of that singular powerful grace that was the privilege of the elect, but for receiving in vain that measure of common grace that they had".[28]

Shedd claims that the distinction between common grace and saving grace is only one of degree not quality. Saving grace is the provision of more help than common grace. He quotes Luke 10:13*f*[29] to show that "grace is to be measured relatively by the result, and not absolutely by a stiff rule which states arithmetically the amount of power exerted. All grace that fails, be it greater or less, is common; all that succeeds, be it greater or less, is special... In order to effect repentance in the people of Tyre, no higher degree [of grace] would have been requisite than that exerted upon Chorazin".[30]

It is on this point that Shedd ties us in knots. He states that the only reason Chorazin didn't turn was because they resisted God's grace. The grace given to Chorazin however would have been sufficient to overcome the resistance of Tyre.[31] He stresses though

---

25. Hodge, *Systematic Theology*, 2:671.
26. Hodge, *Systematic Theology*, 2:675.
27. Shedd, *Dogmatic Theology*, 1:432.
28. Shedd, *Dogmatic Theology*, 1:432.
29. "Woe to you, Chorazin! Woe to you, Bethsaida! For if the mighty works which were done in you had been done in Tyre and Sidon, they would have repented long ago, sitting in sackcloth and ashes. But it will be more tolerable for Tyre and Sidon at the judgment than for you."
30. Shedd, *Dogmatic Theology*, 3:198.
31. Shedd, *Dogmatic Theology*, 3:198.

that this does not mean that Tyre could have "assisted" common grace, in order to make it special,[32] or even have "not resisted".[33] They would still have "resisted", but the common grace given to Chorazin would have overcome the resistance of Tyre and thereby have been special grace.

Berkhof objects to Shedd's denial of a qualitative distinction between common and special grace, insisting that special grace is spiritual, while common grace is natural, affecting only appearances. "No amount of common grace can ever introduce the sinner into the new life that is in Christ Jesus."[34]

It should be pointed out that the terms "common" and "special" are theological, not scriptural terms and so their meaning depends on definition. Nonetheless it would appear that Shedd overlooks the fact that special grace must involve the implanting of a "new heart" in man, something common grace never does. You can't say that "partly giving" a new heart to Chorazin would have been equivalent to "completely giving" a new heart to Tyre. The Canons of Dort 3 & 4.12 make this very plain.

Abraham Kuyper

Abraham Kuyper was a man of parts. "He was not only a dogmatician but also a statesman; he was a professor of theology and prime minister of the queen; he gave learned lectures but also roused men to their political and social duties; Kuyper was educator, journalist, author of many books, orator of great stature, art lover and world traveller."[35] As such he showed the world how to apply his teaching on common grace to everyday life.

He believed that common grace was the source of all culture, and that, as such it had its own independent purpose in "developing creation and making history and culture possible".[36] "This grace is common to the believer and unbeliever and its abuse does not change its gracious character, namely, an unmerited forfeited

32. Shedd, *Dogmatic Theology*, 2:483.
33. Shedd, *Dogmatic Theology*, 3:421.
34. Berkhof, *Systematic Theology*, 439.
35. Henry Van Til, *The Calvinistic Concept of Culture* (Philadelphia: Presbyterian & Reformed, 1972), 117.
36. H. Van Til, *Calvinistic Concept of Culture*, 119.

mercy of God."[37]

"Common grace... gives particular grace a basis for operation" by restraining sin and by providing a culture by means of which the gospel could spread.[38]

Common grace operates at two levels. At the technical and intellectual level culture is advancing. But at the ethical and spiritual level (enabling men to do "moral" good and "civic", i.e. outward, righteousness) common grace is shrinking.[39]

Common grace is not grace apart from Christ. It "[originates] in Christ as the mediator of creation, while particular grace must be ascribed to Christ as mediator of redemption."[40] Kuyper's challenge to the world was: "There is not an inch in the whole area of human existence of which Christ, the sovereign of all, does not cry 'It is mine.'"[41]

Kuyper left the world three large volumes (*De Gemeene Gratie*) which have not yet been translated into English. Cornelius Van Til claims they represent a development in the thought of Kuyper from grace as a restraining influence in society, to grace as a progressive influence on culture in society.[42] These two concepts, we have already noted, were part of Calvin's theology.

Christian Reformed Church

"In 1920 Ralph Janssen, Professor of O.T. at Calvin Seminary, was charged with leanings toward higher criticism. Although he was exonerated by the Synod of that year, charges against him persisted. He retorted that his critics were neglecting the doctrine of common grace, and he quoted Kuyper and Bavinck to that effect, under both of whom he had studied at the Free University of Amsterdam. When he refused to defend himself at the Synod of 1922 because, as he contended, certain members of that Synod had by their denial of common grace disqualified themselves for proper evaluation of his teaching, that body found him guilty as

37. H. Van Til, *Calvinistic Concept of Culture*, 120.
38. H. Van Til, *Calvinistic Concept of Culture*, 121.
39. H. Van Til, *Calvinistic Concept of Culture*, 122.
40. H. Van Til, *Calvinistic Concept of Culture*, 134.
41. H. Van Til, *Calvinistic Concept of Culture*, 117.
42. Cornelius Van Til, *Common Grace* (Philadelphia: P&R 1969), 15*f.*

charged. However, the very next Synod, that of 1924, found two of his most vehement critics Henry Danhof and Herman Hoeksema, guilty of denying the historic Reformed doctrine of common grace."[43]

The Synod of 1924 made the following pronouncement on three points of the doctrine of common grace. It is these three points that have effectively been the centre of the common grace debate since then. I have summarised each, and included the proofs provided by the Synod under the individual point:

1. There is, besides the saving grace of God, shown only to those chosen to eternal life, also a certain favour or grace of God which He shows to His creatures in general.
    - Canons of Dort 2.5, 3 & 4.8,9.
    - Psa. 145:9; Matt. 5:44*f*; Luke 6:35*f*, Acts 14:16*f*; 1 Tim. 4:10; Rom. 2:4; Ezek. 33:11, Ezek. 18:23.
    - Calvin, *Institutes* 2.2.16; Van Mastricht, *First part,* 439.
2. There is a restraint of sin in the life of the individual and in society.
    - Belgic Confession 13, 36.
    - Gen. 6:3; Psa. 81:11*f*, Acts 7:42; Rom. 1:24*ff*; 2 Thes. 2:6*f*.
    - Calvin, *Institutes*, 2.3.3; Van Mastricht, II, 330.
3. The unregenerate, though incapable of any saving good can perform civic righteousness.
    - Canons of Dort 3, 4.4; Belgic Confession.
    - 2 Kings 10:29*f*; 2 Kings 12:2 (2 Chron 24:17*ff*); 2 Kings 14:3 (2 Chron. 25:2,14*ff*); Luke 6:33; Rom. 2:14 (*cf* v13. Rom. 10:5, Gal. 3:12).
    - Ursinus, Schatboek on Lords Day 3; Van Mastricht, I, 458; II, 330.[44]

43. R.B. Kuiper, "Common Grace", *Encyclopaedia of Christianity.* Vol 3. Edited by Edwin Hartshorn Palmer. (Marshallton: The National Foundation for Christian Education, 1972.
44. C. Van Til, *Common Grace*, 19.

Danhof and Hoeksema refused to subscribe to these three points which, they claimed, are pure Arminianism,[45] and as a result they were expelled from the communion of the Christian Reformed Churches.

2. The Goodness of God

The term "common grace" is variously understood by different theologians and, until its definition is more widely accepted it is not the most suitable term to use in this debate.

"Common Grace" Ambiguity

First, what is meant by "common"? By it some mean God's grace to all creatures, some His grace to mankind, and some His grace to all those living under the sway of the gospel.[46] By it others mean "common" as distinct from "special", i.e. natural as opposed to spiritual.[47]

Secondly, the term "grace", in this context is also used loosely. Traditionally "common grace" has been reserved specifically for a work of the Spirit. More recently the term has come also to embrace works of providence in general i.e. "those general blessings such as rain and sunshine, food and drink, clothing and shelter, which God imparts to all men indiscriminately where and in what measure it seems good to Him."[48]

Thirdly, some by "grace" mean the bare undeserved gift of God. Others mean the favourable attitude on God's part that prompted the giving. Berkhof makes a point of stating that "while we sometimes speak of grace as an inherent quality, it is, in reality, the active communication of divine blessings by the inworking of the Holy Spirit".[49] But elsewhere he describes grace as "an attribute of God".

Herman Hoeksema observes that "the term 'grace' as it occurs in Holy Writ itself has many different connotations". Its basic meaning

---

45. G.M. Ophoff, "Anniversary Address" *Standard Bearer* (1st June 1974): 348.
46. Berkhof, *Systematic Theology*, 435.
47. H. Van Til, *Calvinistic Concept of Culture*, 241.
48. Berkhof, *Systematic Theology*, 436.
49. Berkhof, *Systematic Theology*, 427.

is pleasantness. Closely connected are the further implications of a friendly inclination, undeserved favour and the power of God to save. A fifth meaning is simply that of thanks.[50]

I shall use the term "grace" to mean any undeserved favour of God. I will also use it with Berkhof's "double sense"—i.e. referring to God's nature and the gift which proceeds from that nature. In this I am merely following the Scriptures which attribute the same quality to the Giver and the gift (*cf* Gal. 1:15; Eph. 2:8; Tit. 3:4 etc.). There will be none of that logic which can see an act of kindness to man on God's part, but say that it does not necessarily mean that God, in His nature, is kindly disposed towards man in that act. Such an act would never be called kindness.

Grace in Giver and Gift

When Joseph's brothers sold him into Egypt much good came of it, and much prosperity to Joseph. However the nature of the act is to be reckoned from the attitude of the doer, not the benefits or ill received. Therefore although good accrued to Joseph, the act itself was evil, because the brothers were pursuing evil (Gen. 50:20).

Therefore, also, Herman Hoeksema's persistent question "What grace does the reprobate receive in the preaching?"[51] is vain. Grace depends not on the receiver, but the Giver; not upon what use the gift is put to, but upon the attitude of the Giver and the intrinsic usefulness of the gift.

Goodness and Grace

When we speak of God's grace to mankind in general we are dealing with one aspect of what both the Scriptures and the Puritans often dwelt upon: the goodness of God.[52] This is an attribute of God by which He delights to deal bountifully and kindly with all His creatures.[53] It is an inclination of His own nature and therefore necessary. God however is free to manifest His goodness however and whenever

50. Herman Hoeksema, *Reformed Dogmatics* (Grand Rapids: Reformed Free Publishing Association, 1973), 107–112.
51. Engelsma, "'Hyper-Calvinism' and the Call of the Gospel" *Standard Bearer*, 1st October 1974.
52. The Westminster Confession teaches "The light of nature shows that there is a God who is good, and does good unto all" (21.1).
53. Berkhof, *Systematic Theology*, 70; Charnock, *The Existence and Attributes of God*, 541.

He will.

God's goodness is His glory. In Exodus 33:18 Moses besought the Lord to show him His glory. The Lord said, *"I will make all My goodness pass before you, and I will proclaim the name of the Lord before you. I will be gracious to whom I will be gracious, and I will show mercy on whom I will show mercy."* Grace and mercy are two aspects of goodness. To these the Lord adds longsuffering, lovingkindness and truth (Exod. 34:6).

Grace is a principle of God's attribute of goodness whereby He delights to deal with man with a favour he does not deserve.[54] God displays His nature of grace in acts of grace whenever He is good to the sinner.

When God shows men mercy or longsuffering He is displaying His goodness. He is also displaying His grace. The man to whom He is good has forfeited any claim to His mercy or longsuffering. When the Lord shows mercy to the sinner He does so because He is both merciful and gracious. Both principles of His good nature are expressed.

Mercy in itself does not necessarily imply grace. We may show mercy to another, but we rarely entertain the idea that the person we help has forfeited any right to our mercy. Mercy looks only to the need, not to the man in need. God could be a God of mercy, but if He were not a God of grace He would show mercy only to those who had not forfeited their right to it, i.e. to none.

"The favours we receive, are the silver streams which flow from the fountain of God's goodness. This divine attribute of goodness brings in two sorts of blessings. Common blessings: all partake of these, the bad as well as the good; this sweet dew falls upon the thistle as well as the rose. Crowning blessings: these only the godly partake of. 'Who crowneth us with lovingkindness' (Psa. 103:4)".[55]

But how can God punish the creature when by nature He is moved to grace?

God's Grace and Punishment

The Lord continues His revelation to Moses in

54. Berkhof, *Systematic Theology*, 71.
55. Thomas Watson, *A Divine Cordial* (Mulbery: Sovereign Grace Publishers, 1972), 11.

Exodus 34:7, *"...keeping mercy for thousands, forgiving iniquity and transgression and sin, by no means clearing the guilty, visiting the iniquity of the fathers upon the children and the children's children to the third and the fourth generation."*

God's goodness is His glory. But He will not clear the guilty. There is in God a principle of grace. There is also a principle of righteousness. God may refrain from expressing either, but He will not act against one or the other.

In the day He blesses the wicked He expresses His grace. His righteousness is not compromised. But if he eventually left the wicked unpunished, then is His righteousness compromised.

In the day He judges the wicked He expresses His righteousness. His principle of grace is unexpressed, but it is not compromised. He may not give the sinner better than he deserved, but He is certainly giving him no worse. "If God doth not give that good to a creature which it wants by his own demerit, can He be said to wish evil to it or only to deny that goodness which the creature hath forfeited, and which is at God's liberty to retain or disperse?"[56]

God's Benevolence to Mankind

Some theologians speak of God's goodness to mankind under the heading of "love".[57] By it they mean God's inclination to do well to man and to communicate Himself to Him.

Owen defines love as *"velle alicui bonum"* (to will good to any).[58] This is what we mean by God's love toward mankind in general—God pursues (though not uninterruptibly) their wellbeing and provides means intrinsically useful for communicating Himself to them. All acts of God's goodness toward men are acts of love or benevolence and flow from a nature inclined towards benevolence.

Such general benevolence, however, is not the source of salvation. It may well be an encouragement to each and every sinner to turn to God knowing that He is by nature ready to do good to them. But God's benevolence by no means blots out His righteousness and justice, and finally God can only deal with men

56. Charnock, *The Existence and Attributes of God*, 555.
57. Berkhof, *Systematic Theology*, 71.
58. Owen, *The Death of Death*, 208.

as they justly deserve.

God can show love and grace to mankind, but He cannot save him unless atonement be provided. Such atonement could only be by means of the shame and humiliation of the Son, the Second Person of the Trinity, whom the Father loved from eternity. God's benevolence and grace which moved Him to deal bountifully with even fallen man, did not move Him to make **such** a sacrifice for all men who had so arrogantly and wickedly rebelled against Him.

Neither did God's abhorrence at the death of man move Him to make such a sacrifice.[59]

God's Special Love for the Elect[60]

For some reason, unknown to us, God, in eternity set His love particularly upon a people. "God's thoughts and ways of mercy are infinitely above ours; His reasons are all fetched from within himself, and not from anything in us."[61] By His eternal decree He determined to seek their good at all times. His love for us was so intense and His decree of election so unalterable that He was moved to send His own Son to be crucified at our hands that He might save us (John 3:16). This atonement met the demands of His righteousness and satisfied His strict justice.

Owen is quite right when he says, "That love which was the cause of the sending or giving of Christ" was not God's "natural propensity to the good of all" but a "most eminent act" of God's will of "love and favour to the creature.".[62] "It is most false which by some is said—that special grace flows from that which they call general grace, and special mercy from general mercy. There is a whole nest of mistakes in that conception. God's sovereign distinguishing will is the fountain of all special grace and mercy."[63]

59. While the principles of sovereign love, and of delight in the sinner turning, were not the sole sufficient cause of the atonement, there is no doubt that they found expression in the atonement.
60. James MacGregor, "The Free Offer in the Westminster Confession", *Banner of Truth Magazine* (July-August 1970): 57. MacGregor distinguishes God's "philanthropy" (general love towards mankind) from His *agape* (special love for elect). Such a distinction is common in Reformed theology.
61. Henry, *Commentary*, 1467.
62. Owen, *The Death of Death*, 208.
63. Owen, "The Strength of Faith", 44.

That "whole nest of mistakes" hatched Arminianism and Amyraldianism.

Is it simply adding to the confusion to speak of a benevolent love and an electing love? There is no reason why this should be so. We love our children. We also love those whom we don't know who are in need in other lands, and show it by aiding them as we are able.[64] Anyone can understand such a distinction—a distinction which is quite Scriptural. One is described in 1 John 3:1 as an intense, jealous care. The other is spoken of in Matthew 5:44–45, 48 as a benevolent care.

Benevolent Love and Electing Love

It should be clearly understood that benevolence is not an attitude of God towards the reprobate as a class, in the same way that electing love is an attitude of God towards the elect as a class. Benevolence is an attitude of God towards men as a class, which includes both elect and reprobate. Man as a creature is the object of God's benevolence.

The question is always asked "How can God be favourably inclined toward a man, and at the same time be filled with hatred against him, so that He damns that man for ever?"[65]

Love of Reprobate?

I have already partly answered this question by demonstrating that there is nothing inconsistent in a God of grace and justice doing good to a man, but then punishing him for his sin.

There are other questions to be answered:

- Can God both love and hate at the same time?
- Would not this be inconsistent with His simplicity?
- Can God be benevolent toward those whom He hates from eternity?
- Would not this be inconsistent with His immutability?

Before answering these questions let us be clear as to what we

64. Of course I am not suggesting our children are the "elect" and those in other lands are not; I am just demonstrating that, even in human experience, there are different types and degrees of love. D. A. Carson, *The Difficult Doctrine of the Love of God* (Wheaton: Crossway, 2000) and D. A. Carson, *Love in Hard Places* (Wheaton: Crossway, 2002).
65. H. C. Hoeksema, "O.P.C. and the 'Free Offer'", 1st January 1974.

mean by "love" and "hate". When we say "God is love" we mean (among other things) that God is moved by His nature to deal bountifully with the creature (i.e. *velle alicui bonum*). If God is moved thus by any righteousness in the creature we call this "pleasurable love" (or "love of complacency"[66]). It is the result of God's goodness welling up through His righteousness and taking delight in the reflection of His own character in the creature. God may be moved (at least, in part) to such love towards the Christian living a holy life.

Love and Hate

If, on the other hand, there is no such cause in the creature then God's love is sovereign love. God's goodness is displayed through grace. Such is God's benevolence to men in general. And such, above all else, is His peculiar love towards His elect which goes well beyond any delight He takes in a holy life.

In a similar manner we may speak of God's hate in terms of a revulsion in His nature towards someone, thereby being moved to bring misery upon them. If He is moved by the unrighteousness of the creature, such hatred is judicial, and is the complement of pleasurable love.

Can hatred also be sovereign? Strictly speaking, no! God may love where there is nothing loveable, but He will never hate where there is nothing hateable.

Preterition is the only form of sovereign "hate" spoken of in Scripture. Romans 9:11 refers to God's "hatred" of Esau when he had done "neither good nor evil"—it is a sovereign act. It refers to God's preterition of Esau for no other reason than His good pleasure. It is "not doing" what He did for Jacob. "Jacob have I loved, Esau have I loved not". Shedd makes this point.[67]

Such preterition says nothing about God's attitude towards those passed over (except that they are not going to be loved with God's electing love), nor about their destiny. "Were not all men sinners there might still be an election, as sovereign as now; and there being an election, there would still be as sovereign a rejection: but the rejection would not be a rejection to punishment, to destruction,

66. B. B. Warfield, "God's Immeasurable Love", *Biblical and Theological Studies* (Philadelphia: Presbyterian & Reformed, 1968), 515.

67. Shedd, *Dogmatic Theology*, 1:447.

to eternal death, but to some other destiny consonant to the state in which those passed by should be left. It is not indeed, then, because men are sinners that men are left unelected; election is free, and its obverse of rejection must be equally free: but it is solely because men are sinners that what they are left to is destruction."[68]

This is the position of the Westminster Confession: a sovereign preterition, and a judicial condemnation. It is not sufficient simply to claim that, since God decreed in eternity to pour out His wrath upon Esau, before he was even born, therefore His displeasure was sovereign, not judicial (see my comments on the Westminster Confession in Chapter 1 "Historical Survey"). Strictly speaking, hatred is always judicial and always takes into account sin. Eternal hatred (other than sovereign preterition) is based on the eternal decree of sin.

2 Thessalonians 2:10–12 speaks of God's damnation of the reprobate (*"those who perish"*) whose sin brings upon them further delusions from God and hence greater condemnation. The cause of their condemnation was to be found in that *"they did not receive the love of the truth, that they might be saved"*, which God foreordained but did not originate. *"Deus non est ultor illius rei cuius est auctor; sed Deus est ultor cordis obdurati."* ("God is not the punisher of what He is the author; but God is the punisher of the hard heart" attributed to Fulgentius by Aquinas.)

Even Gomarus, a supralapsarian and outspoken critic of Arminius asked for the floor but once at Dort to refute the suggestion of an absolute predestination apart from any consideration of man's sin.[69] Dort responded by rejecting any notion "that God, by a mere arbitrary act of His will, without the least respect or view to any sin, has predestinated the greatest part of the world to eternal damnation, and has created them for this very purpose".[70]

Is it possible for God to love (sovereignly) those whom He hates (judicially)?

Can God Love and Hate?

Psalm 5:5 says that God *"hates all workers of*

68. B. B. Warfield, "Predestination", *Biblical and Theological Studies* (Philadelphia: Presbyterian & Reformed, 1968), 317.
69. Kistemaker as cited in DeJong, *Crisis*, 43.
70. Canons of the Synod of Dort, Conclusion.

iniquity." H. C. Hoeksema quotes this passage, along with many similar verses concerning God's hate of the wicked, to prove that God cannot love the reprobate: "For the sake of the argument, we will not even use the term reprobate but simply speak of the wicked."[71] But why does he exclude the elect in their wickedness from this verse? God "hates" the wicked (in Psa. 5:5) though he be among the elect. In this case "hate", while not with an aim at the person's destruction (since God ultimately aims at his salvation), nonetheless manifests itself in a genuine revulsion in God's nature towards that person in his wickedness.

Ephesians 2 clearly states that we were all once *"dead in trespasses and sins"* and we all *"were by nature children of wrath,* ***just as the others****"*—all of us identified with all other *"workers of iniquity." "The wrath of God abides on anyone"* as long as *"he does not believe in the Son,* (John 3:36), including all of us until we come to faith in Christ. God *"hates all workers of iniquity"*, yet He has loved His elect with an everlasting love from long before they believe. And even believers, when they backslide, may feel God's anger, wrath, and displeasure (Psa. 6:1, 30:4f, 38:1, 90:7; Prov. 6:16*ff*; Jonah 4:1–8) —while, at the same time, God loves them with an everlasting love.

James Fergusson sums it up: "Though God love His elect, even in their unregenerate state, with an everlasting love, Eph. 1:4, yet so long as they are unrenewed, and have not fled to Christ by faith, He cannot adjudge them to eternal life, or look upon them any other way than as men under an actual obligation to lie under the curse of the law, which is eternal wrath: so 'they are enemies.'"[72]

This is the glory of God's love—that He could love with such great love those of us whom He finds, in ourselves, hateful and repulsive. I remember how starkly this dawned upon me after a fellow rang me up in the darkest hour of the night, and I sat with him till the sun rose as he, in heartfelt repentance, poured out a catalogue of one horrible sin after another. As I drove home in first light, sickened by what I had just heard, it dawned on me how God must see all our sins as even more horrible, repulsive and hateful

71. H. C. Hoeksema, "O.P.C. and the 'Free Offer'", 1st April 1974.
72. J. Fergusson, *The Epistles of Paul 1659–74* (London: Banner of Truth, 1978.), 339. Note Fergusson's comment on Col. 1:21.

than I saw this poor man's. And yet, He loves us! *"God demonstrates His own love toward us, in that while we were still sinners, Christ died for us."* (Rom. 5:8) Yes, us!—who are all *"by nature children of wrath, **just as the others**".* "Foul I to the fountain fly"!

It is not enough to mouth the cliché that God loves the sinner, but hates the sin. No, God *"hates all workers of iniquity"* themselves. There is a sense that God hates, i.e. feels the utmost revulsion, when we, even as redeemed sinners, work iniquity.

There is therefore no reason to suppose that God cannot sovereignly love and pursue the welfare of one who at the same time is hateful. In fact this very truth is taught in Matthew 5 where we are taught to follow God's example and love (Matt. 5:44*f*) those whom we nevertheless find hateful because they are *"evil"* (Psa. 139:21; Prov. 8:13; 2 Chron. 19:2 *f*). "Just as God can consistently display his wrath upon the objects of his everlasting love, so he can, and does, display abundant tokens of his love of benevolence on those who are objects of his everlasting hate."[73]

Benevolence and God's Simplicity

It is not inconsistent with God's simplicity that He should love and hate at the same time. He is not expressing the same in opposite directions. Rather He is expressing love/hate through two principles. His love wells up through grace, His hate is the response of His righteousness.

Because His love is sovereign it is independent of His hate—or how else would we have ever been saved? On the other hand His hate is judicial and contingent (in His decree) upon the creature's unrighteousness. These two principles do not contradict one another. They are complementary in God's simple nature.

Benevolence and Hatred from Eternity

H.C. Hoeksema insists that the case of the reprobate leaves no room for any love since God's hatred of them is from eternity.[74] But he has forgotten the distinction, which in another place he himself draws attention to[75], between preterition and precondemnation.

73. Andrew Swanson, "The Doctrine of Reprobation and Its Practical Implications" *Banner of Truth Magazine*, November 1976, 21.
74. H. C. Hoeksema, "Question Box".
75. H. C. Hoeksema, "O.P.C. and the 'Free Offer'", 15th September 1973.

I am amazed at Hoeksema's double mindedness on this question. There is no doubt that he agrees that the only reason that the ordination of the reprobate to dishonour and wrath was for their sin.[76] And yet in another place he ascribes the reason for God's wrath to His sovereign displeasure!—He says that God's "hatred" of Esau (which is sovereign preterition) "reveals itself in a manifestation of wrath against the people who were the objects of God's sovereign displeasure".[77]

But God is never malevolent. He never hates without cause. His wrath never arises from sovereign displeasure but only from judicial displeasure. "If God hate any, it is because they first hated him."[78] God's hatred is not malevolency (hatred without cause) but holiness (hatred with cause). The reason God *"laid waste the heritage of Esau"* (Mal. 1:3) was not because He had passed him by, but because, when Esau had been passed by, he who had been foreordained to become *"the Territory of Wickedness"* was found to be deserving *"the indignation of the Lord"* (Mal. 1:4).

"While sovereignty alone accounts for the love of God towards Jacob, and indeed towards everyone of his elect, the same does not hold good for God's hatred of Esau or any of the non-elect. By nature all mankind deserves the eternal hatred of God. God in his sovereign choice of a people from such material finds no cause in the objects of his choice for the love he grants them. His love is sovereign, free and an unconditional gift. While it is true that God sovereignly withholds his [electing] love from the non-elect it does not follow that he sovereignly hates them. He hates them because they are hateful and he has sovereignly determined to withhold the grace which alone could change this hatefulness."[79]

Some will object to the proposition that God will at one time manifest benevolence and at another time cease to do so (as in the final judgment of the reprobate). This surely contradicts His immutability. Rodman cannot accept that "in the inscrutable counsel of God's will, He loves the elect with an everlasting love,

Benevolence and God's Immutability

76. H. C. Hoeksema, "O.P.C. and the 'Free Offer'", 15th September 1973.
77. H. C. Hoeksema, "Question Box".
78. Henry, *Commentary*, 1464.
79. Swanson, "Doctrine of Reprobation", 21*f.*

while His love for the reprobate is partial and changeable".[80]

In answering him we present a number of considerations:

1. First, any argument about God's immutability begins with God's nature, not its manifestation. God's nature of holiness demands the punishment of all sin—that of the elect and that of the reprobate, irrespective of any benevolent nature in God. That God punishes the sin of the elect in Christ, does not deny a nature moved to sovereign love. So too, God's punishment of the sin of the reprobate in the reprobate does not deny a nature moved to sovereign benevolence.

   Why holiness should deny benevolence I know not. And to presume that, once God has manifested His principle of sovereign benevolence to the reprobate He is then obliged to continue to manifest it uninterruptedly, denies not only His freedom to express His principles, but also the sovereignty of His benevolence.

2. Some will object, though, that we then have no reason to assume that God's sovereign love to the elect will not cease. If it is only God's nature that is immutable and necessary, and not the free expression of that nature, how can even the elect be certain that God will not cease to love them?

   However the uninterrupted kindness of God towards the elect is based, not merely on God's inclination to deal bountifully with mankind but on an eternal act of God's will, "even that act of His will which was the cause of sending His Son Jesus Christ".[81]

   When we say our confidence is in the immutability of God we do not mean that there is an obligation on God's part to manifest sovereign love simply because it is His nature. God is free to express His nature however and whenever He will—to manifest benevolence toward us or withhold it.

   But our confidence is in God's immutability, in that, once He has decreed that all things will *"work together for the good to those who are called according to His purpose"* (Rom.

80. Rodman, "*The Desire of God for the Salvation of the Reprobate*", 30.
81. Owen, *The Death of Death*, 208.

8:28) He will not alter that decree. He has decreed to love us invariably—this is our confidence. Our assurance is that God who *"from the beginning chose us **for salvation**"* (2 Thes. 2:13) will see His purpose accomplished and His elect saved.

Only the elect can have this confidence. Mankind in general (reprobate and unconverted) may experience the benevolence of God, but this is no reason for them to assume that God will never cease to manifest His benevolence towards them.

Only the converted can bask in the security of the love of God. For God's love for such was so intense that He gave His own Son. Any lesser gift would be no cause to assume that God would also give him all things. But *"He who did not spare His own Son, but delivered Him up for us all, how shall He not with Him also freely give us all things"* (Rom. 8:32). Notice that God's continuing to bless us is still "free". But the logic is inescapable. If He gave us His own Son, what further evidence do we need that God's benevolence will never cease toward us?

The unbeliever cannot say this. He cannot say, for instance, "He that showed us His kindness and mercy in everyday blessings, how shall He not freely give us all things?" What Paul is saying in Romans 8:32 is that any other act of mercy that we have received is no assurance that God's acts of mercy towards us will never cease. The only act of mercy that inevitably gives us such confidence is the gift of His Son.

To God alone be the glory! Shall His love ever cease toward us?

3. Dabney argues that God must have been moved to compassion for Esau, as well as Jacob, since His nature is bent towards compassion. "God's optional liberty is not whether He shall *have* the propensions of His essential principles but whether He shall *execute* them by His volitions".[82] Similarly God would have been moved towards a righteous rejection of sinful Jacob, the same way as He was moved to reject

82. Dabney, "God's Indiscriminate Proposals of Mercy", 303.

Esau. But for a reason unknown,[83] God acted upon His compassion, not His righteousness towards Jacob, and upon His righteousness, not His compassion, towards Esau.

This is what we said before—that God's nature is necessary and the way God expresses that nature within himself by delighting or delighting not in contingent events is necessary. But how He will express His nature outside of Himself in the decree, He is perfectly free.

Dabney goes on to assert that God's compassion toward the reprobate is not left unexpressed, but is directed toward a subordinate end, the mitigation of his punishment (presumably by acts of "common grace").

With this I basically agree. But I deny that this is a lesser end than that to which God could have directed it. God could not, on the grounds of compassion alone, have done more for the reprobate without compromising His holiness. It is therefore wrong to imagine that God, by His compassion, aims at much but satisfies Himself with little. He expressed His compassion as much as He wished to, in the reprobate. It was only because of a greater principle unknown to us, which He expressed in choosing His elect, that He was able to show them greater compassion.

Compassion (a principle constituting God's benevolence) is not an ultimate or sufficient cause for the salvation of sinners.

Significance of History

Those that deny the reality of God's kindness to the reprobate are in danger of turning life into a dream in which "life is a tale, told by an idiot, full of sound and fury, signifying nothing".[84]

This is a danger, inherent in supralapsarianism, which ignores the significance of means and only looks to the end. Engelsma denies that supralapsarianism has any bearing upon the question.[85] But

83. A prior reason would have been His decree of election and preterition. The ultimate reason for election and preterition is however unknown.

84. William Shakespeare, *Macbeth* Act 5, scene 5.

85. Engelsma, "'Hyper-Calvinism' and the Call of the Gospel", 1st June 1974.

only a supralapsarian could consistently ask, "How can God be favourably inclined toward a man that He will damn forever". All he can see is the reprobate as if he were already in hell and the elect already in heaven. Everything is interpreted in the light of this. Nothing has significance apart from this.

"In what light must we consider the things which in this life the godly and ungodly have in common?... In the light of eternity. All things of the present life are but means to an eternal end... But" (one may object) "can we not truly say that God bestows the things of the present time upon the ungodly in His grace, though the wicked employ them unto their own destruction?... It is certainly true that the wicked with all the means at their command serve sin and work out their own destruction, yet, it is equally true that they do so in full harmony with God's counsel and under His providence."[86] This seems to satisfy Herman Hoeksema that no more need be said regarding the possibility of God's kindness to the reprobate in this life. He will one day be in hell, and that by God's decree—so what's the point of speaking about kindness having any significance now!

Cornelius Van Til warns that we are not to be "like the impatient disciples [Luke 9:54] [anticipating] the course of history and [dealing] with men as though they were already that which by God's eternal decree they one day will be."[87]

The reprobate will eventually suffer the same punishment as the devil and his angels. But to none of these reprobate angels does God grant a dispensation of longsuffering. God never offered the devil salvation if he repented. God only makes that offer to man. Therefore, to regard the reprobate (whoever he may be) as already in hell is to tell God that HIS-story is without significance. Their reprobation may be certain, but it is not yet complete.

So too, our salvation is certain, but it is not yet complete. We are still sinners (1 John 1:10), we still have sin in our nature (1 John 1:8), we are still subject to God's anger at times (Psa. 90:7). But there will come a time when this will be no more.

86. Herman Hoeksema, *The Protestant Reformed Churches in America* (Grand Rapids: First Protestant Reformed Church, 1947), 322*f.*

87. C. Van Til, *Common Grace*, 83.

For the reprobate also, there will come a time when he will no longer live under God's longsuffering. He will no longer be a recipient of God's benevolence, but only of His justice.

It cannot be denied that history is a process of differentiation, sorting out the elect from the reprobate. God has decreed that it will take many thousands of years to effect what was accomplished in a moment in the angelic world. This does not deny the significance of history, but rather underscores it. How else is man's utter depravity better (or worse) manifested than in his rejection of God's grace and kindness? "Providence is not pure prolongation, or merely scaffolding for the building of special grace, but God displays His longsuffering mercy and goodness in history."[88] Charles Hodge quotes Dr. Candlish to the effect that "the entire history of the human race, from the apostasy to the final judgment, is a dispensation of forbearance in respect to the reprobate, in which many blessings, physical and moral, affecting their characters and destinies forever, accrue even to the heathen."[89]

The final judgment of the reprobate will be that God showed him kindness, real kindness, and yet he failed to respond. "God is justified in the denial of His special grace to those who do not make a due use of His common gifts and grace; and indeed here will lie men's damnation, because they do not make a just use of that common grace which they have, and might make a better use of it than they do."[90]

Some will be beaten with few stripes. Although they deserved none of God's kindness, yet they were shown a little. Others will be beaten with many stripes (Luke 12:48). Unto them much was given: God's kindness was showered upon them. These acts of kindness upon God's part were not "bare facts and events" sent merely to bring about their fate. "It were impossible that [the reprobate's] punishment should be increased by his manipulation of the facts about him, unless these facts were evidence of the undeserved favour of God in relation to him."[91] To interpret God's

88. H. Van Til, *Calvinistic Concept of Culture*, 234.
89. Berkhof, *Systematic Theology*, 438.
90. Poole, *Annotations*, 3:249.
91. Cornelius Van Til, *Particularism and Common Grace* (Lewis J Grotenhuis, 1951), 13.

"kindness" in a purely mechanical way as a means to an end is to divorce providence from morality. God becomes no more than the Grand Puppet Master.

The man beaten with many stripes is judged more severely, not just because he manipulated a different set of facts, but because these "facts" he manipulated were mercies from a merciful God. "Abused goodness turns into the greater severity."[92]

3. The Testimony of Scripture

We now come to a consideration of texts variously used to establish the doctrine of common grace. These include passages that teach God's preservation of individual men, His providence, His general benevolence, His acts of mercy and kindness, His longsuffering and restraint of sin in the individual and the revelation of His character to man together with the offer of salvation to those who repent.

Preservation, Providence and General Benevolence

God's goodness or love consists first in a principle whereby He delights to provide for and preserve His creation. God manifests this principle in His provision. God is not obliged to provide for men, especially since the fall. That He does so is pure grace.That He sometimes refrains from doing so does not deny His grace. If it did His provision would not be grace.

We may ask, what is the purpose of such grace? One ultimate purpose is to leave men inexcusable. But, as we have seen, if grace were not truly kindness it would leave men no more inexcusable than before. Rather we must admit that, during this dispensation, God freely (i.e. by what means and at what time He is pleased) pursues the well-being of men. He pursues their physical well-being, He pursues the communication of His nature with them, and He pursues their salvation.[93]

92. Henry, *Commentary*, 1491.

93. I use the term "pursue" in preference to "seek" because the latter implies a determination to see an end accomplished. God pursues man's physical well-being, salvation etc. by providing means that are intrinsically useful for

When we say that God freely shows His goodness from time to time and place to place, we do not mean to imply that He bestows His grace sparingly. The Psalmist exclaims: *"The earth is full of the goodness of the Lord"* (Psa. 33:5), and again *"The Lord is good to all, and His tender mercies are over all His works"* (Psa. 145:9). Herman Hoeksema wrote off the plain meaning of this verse by saying it is an isolated text[94] that cannot be taken at face value in the light of God's punishment of the wicked (Psa. 73, Psa. 92).[95] But there is

---

accomplishing that end. Whether man uses these means for his own well-being or for his destruction, alters not a jot the kindness of God in providing the means (*cf.* Hosea 2:8).

If any object that we ought not conceive of God pursuing but not attaining, he should reflect that this is a purely philosophical objection. The same objection can be brought against the ruin of a perfect creation, or the abandoning of the (physical) nation of Israel, or God's longsuffering of the reprobate (Rom. 9:22), or His waiting for such men *"in the hope that they might grope for Him and find Him"* (Acts 17:27). To everything there is a purpose.

94. H. C. Hoeksema, "O.P.C. and the 'Free Offer'", 15th May 1973.
95. It is interesting that H. C. Hoeksema uses the same "isolated text" reasoning to dismiss the meaning of Matt. 5:44–48 (H. C. Hoeksema, "Question Box", 1st June 1974). One wonders how many isolated passages there can be before they are no longer isolated.

I am reminded of the young student for the ministry who declared that he did not think the Virgin Birth had to be regarded as true because it was only revealed in a single (!) passage. A godly minister of the presbytery examining him, asked how many times he thought God should reveal a truth before he was obliged to accept it.

It is interesting also that the hyper-calvinists (from whom Herman Hoeksema dissociates himself) established their case by "isolated text" reasoning. Article 32 (1st Part) of the Gospel Standard Churches seeks to justify its position by saying: "We believe that it would be unsafe, from the brief records we have of the way in which the apostles, under the immediate direction of the Lord, addressed their hearers in certain special cases and circumstances, to derive absolute and universal rules for ministerial address in the present day under widely different circumstances." (https://www.gospelstandard.org.uk/GospelStandard/media/gs/Articles.pdf).

H. C. Hoeksema often insists that issues are to be decided, not upon the "superficial sound" of a "few texts" but upon the "current teaching" of Scripture (H. C. Hoeksema, "O.P.C. and the 'Free Offer'", 15th January 1974, 1st April 1974 and 1st May 1974). He then produces nineteen texts which show that God hates the "wicked" (or, by a superficial switch, the "reprobate"), and proceeds to state that no further explanation is needed (1st April 1974). He triumphantly adds that his passages "outnumber" those cited by Murray and Stonehouse (1st May 1974).

nothing contradictory in God's benevolence to the wicked and His punishment of them, as we have seen.

Many commentators,[96] as well as others like Charnock[97] see no reason why the "[wicked's] sin and depravity should prevent God from showering down His goodness upon them" (Calvin). Such goodness is manifested to all that live in this dispensation, "to all but devils and damned sinners, that have shut themselves out from His goodness".[98]

Two other passages are often quoted:

> Matt. 5:44–45,48 *"Love your enemies, bless those who curse you, do good to those who hate you, and pray for those who spitefully use you and persecute you, that you may be sons of your Father in heaven; for He makes His sun rise on the evil and on the good, and sends rain on the just and on the unjust... Therefore you shall be perfect, just as your Father in heaven is perfect."*

> Luke 6:35–36 *"Love your enemies, do good, and lend, hoping for nothing in return; and your reward will be great, and you will be sons of the Most High. For He is kind to the unthankful and evil. Therefore be merciful, just as your Father also is merciful."*

Here God enjoins us to be like Him—to show love to the unlovely because He does the same. If we are to be like God we are to emulate His attribute of sovereign love, and love those whom we have no cause to love, and whom we, even like God, hate for their sin. But even our hate must be like God's, a "judicial" hate. We are not to be malevolent, hating, without cause (Matt. 5:22).

We have no mandate, of course, to emulate God's judgment of the wicked. That is His prerogative alone (Luke 6:37). But Calvin says we are to emulate His "fatherly goodness and liberality.... None are the children of God but those who resemble Him in gentleness and kindness". God's "divine kindness" is "common to all"; His "rain and sunshine" are but a "synecdoche, [including] a

96. Calvin, *Commentary on the Book of Psalms* (Edinburgh, Calvin Translation Society, 1849), 5:276; Poole, *Annotations*, 2:210.
97. Charnock, *The Existence and Attributes of God*, 543.
98. Matthew Henry, *Commentary*, 948 c.f. C. Van Til, *Common Grace*, 30.

vast number of other favours".[99] Matthew Poole does not hesitate to point out that God's mercies are evidence of His "common love, which He extendeth to all mankind".[100] Henry comments in a similar vein.[101] Berkhof,[102] Murray,[103] Murray and Stonehouse,[104] Hulse,[105] Cornelius Van Til,[106] Henry Van Til,[107] R. B. Kuiper,[108] and G. H. Clark[109] are all of the same mind.

H. C. Hoeksema flatly rejects such an interpretation, though he again exhibits double mindedness. He does not deny that God sends gifts upon the reprobate (Matt. 5:45). These however are bare acts of providence and do not proceed from the kindness of God's nature.[110]

Such a view presents a problem. For the parallel passage in Luke 6:35 (which Calvin, by the way, exegetes in conjunction with Matt. 5:44) speaks of God being "kind" and "merciful" to the "evil". Now it would be absurd to try and separate an act of kindness from an attitude of kindness. H. C. Hoeksema has a solution. God, in Luke, is not talking about kindness to all men generally but to only the unconverted elect.[111] In this he will have his cake and eat it too. For at one time the "wicked" (whom God hates) can refer only to the reprobate,[112] but now the "evil" can refer only to the elect.

Therefore H. C. Hoeksema concludes that Matthew 5 and Luke 6 present two unconnected reasons for showing love to our enemies. The first is that God provides (without love) for all men, and the second is that God shows love to the unconverted elect.

99. Calvin, *Matthew, Mark, and Luke*, 1:307.
100. Poole, *Annotations*, 3:26.
101. Henry, *Commentary*, 1483.
102. Berkhof, *Systematic Theology*, 446.
103. John Murray, "The Atonement and the Free Offer of the Gospel" *Banner of Truth Magazine,* Jul-Aug 1968.
104. Murray and Stonehouse, *The Free Offer of the Gospel*, 5.
105. Hulse, *The Free Offer*, 7.
106. C. Van Til, *Common Grace*, 13.
107. H. Van Til, *Calvinistic Concept of Culture*, 234.
108. Kuiper, *The Bible Tells Us So,* 65; Kuiper, "Common Grace", 50.
109. Clark, *Biblical Predestination*, 132.
110. H. C. Hoeksema, "O.P.C. and the 'Free Offer'", 15th January 1974.
111. H. C. Hoeksema, "O.P.C. and the 'Free Offer'", 15th September 1973 c.f. H.C. Hoeksema, "Question Box" *Standard Bearer,* 1st June 1974.
112. H. C. Hoeksema, "O.P.C. and the 'Free Offer'", 1st April 1974.

But to read into God's provision an attitude of love is unwarranted (i.e. unwarranted in Matthew not in Luke).[113]

The position of the Evangelical Presbyterian Church of Australia (E.P.C.A.) is not entirely clear. On the one hand they speak of "temporal blessings" and "mercies" on the part of God towards the whole of creation. But they say these "can only refer to the works of God's providence in respect of time, and cannot include grace and favour".[114] Hoeksema astutely points out that "they do not explain what this mercy is, neither how it can exclude grace and favour".[115] Is God's mercy towards men in general deserved or undeserved? It must be one or the other. The E.P.C.A. equivocate.

They do not deny that God is good to all but state that any "temporal blessings" are not "indicative of His love and longsuffering in redemption toward the non-elect, and a desire in Him that they might be saved".[116]

I agree that temporal blessings are not indicative of God's elective love but I reaffirm that they are evidence of a sovereign benevolence toward men whereby He pursues their physical and spiritual well-being. This is more clearly taught in the following passages:

> Acts 14:16–17 "[God], *in bygone generations allowed all nations to walk in their own ways. Nevertheless He did not leave Himself without witness, in that He did good, gave us rain from heaven and fruitful seasons, filling our hearts with food and gladness."*
>
> Acts 17:25–27 "[God] *gives to all life, breath, and all things. And He has made from one blood every nation of men to dwell on all the face of the earth, and has determined their preappointed times and the boundaries of their dwellings, so that they should seek the Lord, in the hope that they might grope for Him and find Him."*

113. That many acts of God's providence are kindness is evident from Matt. 6:25–34, 10:29–31; Prov. 29:13; Hos. 2:8.
114. H. C. Hoeksema, "The E.P.C. and Common Grace" *Standard Bearer,* 15th December 1974.
115. H. C. Hoeksema, "The E.P.C. and Common Grace", 15th December 1974.
116. Rodman, *Universalism and the Reformed Churches*, 8, 12.

Here the text specifically states that God's gifts are "good". Herman Hoeksema denies this, saying they are not for the good of the reprobate.[117]

We see also that the intrinsic usefulness of God's gifts of providence is that they are designed to move us to seek the Lord. It is in this light that we should view their immediate purpose as springing from the kindness of God. "The good things which [God] gave them, and the patience whereby He spared them, were no arguments of an implacable disposition, and therefore of a disposition willing to be appeased".[118]

The preceding arguments are summed up in:

> 1 Tim. 4:10 *"God is the Saviour of all men, especially of those that believe".*

Many expositors translate "Saviour" (σωτήρ) as "Preserver" instead of "Saviour". This is legitimate, though it should be borne in mind that the "special" preservation of believers is salvation.

The verse expresses that principle in God's nature whereby He delights to preserve and provide for His creation. God therefore pursues man's preservation, including its highest form in salvation. In the elect alone He has determined to pursue it to the end.

Acts of Mercy and Kindness

God's acts of mercy flow from a merciful principle in God whereby He delights in acts of mercy and kindness.

> Psa. 145:8 *"The Lord is gracious and full of compassion, slow to anger, and great in mercy".*

We are reminded that God can show sovereign love, but He does not show sovereign anger. Luke 6:35 teaches that God is *"kind to the unthankful and to the evil".* Whereas Psalm 145 refers simply to God's nature, Luke 6 refers to the manifestation of that nature, even to the evil.

We should not split God's love for the reprobate by assuming that He pursues their physical well-being by the blessings of common

117. Herman Hoeksema, *The Protestant Reformed Churches in America*, 328.

118. Charnock, *The Existence and Attributes of God*, 783. See also Murray and Stonehouse, *The Free Offer of the Gospel*, 8 and C. Van Til, *Common Grace*, 33.

grace but not their spiritual well-being. To say that it is not God's ultimate purpose to save the reprobate is no argument against God's pursuing their salvation. Shall we say that God was not pursuing Israel's physical well-being (Hos. 2:8), simply because it was His ultimate purpose to take away her supply (Hos. 2:9)? Of course not. God's kindness is exhibited through the intrinsic usefulness of the bounty supplied, not the use or misuse/abuse of that gift by the receiver.

Christ shows the compassion of God pursuing salvation when He is approached by the rich young ruler. This man came enquiring after eternal life. And Jesus, *"looking at him loved him"* (Mark 10:21). To say it was a compassion regarding temporal mercies only is ridiculous. Christ's love and compassion had in view the man's salvation, even though He had not that intense love toward him which He reserves for the elect. Christ pursued the man's salvation, but (as far as we can tell) He had no intention of pursuing it to accomplishment.

In Luke 7:30 we see that God may pursue a purpose (βουλή) of repentance (i.e. as signified in baptism) and salvation without any intention of accomplishing it. "God from all eternity purposed to give the Jews the ministry of John the Baptist and Christ, as means for their salvation, not which should be certainly effective of it, but that should have such a tendency towards it, as without their own refusing, and opposing them, it should have been effective, and was in their own nature" [i.e. intrinsically] "a proper means in order to it". The reprobate reject such a purpose "against themselves". "Take it as God's act, it was towards themselves, that is, for their good; if we refer it to their act of rejection, or refusal, it was against themselves, a judging of themselves unworthy of eternal life".[119]

That the goodness and mercy of God are intrinsically useful to lead to salvation is evident from:

> <u>Rom. 2:4–5</u> *"Do you despise the riches of His goodness, forbearance, and longsuffering, not knowing that the goodness of God leads you to repentance? But in accordance with your hardness and your impenitent heart you are treasuring up for yourself wrath in the day of wrath and revelation of the*

119. Poole, *Annotations*, 3:217.

righteous judgment of God."

Verse 5 makes it plain that this passage is applicable to the reprobate. Matthew Henry says: "The consideration of the goodness of God, His common goodness to all (the goodness of His providence, of His patience and of His offers) should be effectual to bring us all to repentance; and the reason why so many continue in impenitency is, because they do not know and consider this."[120] See similar comments by Calvin,[121] Haldane,[122] Poole,[123] and Thomas Chalmers.[124] Also Charnock,[125] Shedd,[126] and Berkhof[127].

Herman Hoeksema is the only one to split verse 4 from verse 5, saying that "the goodness of God that leads us to repentance" refers "only to the elect".[128] That God's goodness is effectual in leading only the elect to repentance, none deny. But to say that it has no reference to these who, by abusing it, store up *"wrath in the day of wrath"* is absurd.

"Let grace be shown to the wicked, yet he will not learn righteousness" (Isa. 26:10).

Longsuffering and Restraint of Sin

The exercise of God's patience flows from a nature which is longsuffering. In this especially we see that we live in a dispensation of grace.

What Calvin saw in the 16th century is true of this whole age. "In our own day, though He has experienced a marvellous depravity in the world, He still continues to dispense His grace."[129] Even the Old Testament was a dispensation of longsuffering to the wicked. God *"suffered all nations to walk in their own ways"* (Acts 14:16),

120. Henry, *Commentary*, 2196.
121. Calvin, *Romans,* 87–89.
122. Robert Haldane, *Exposition of the Epistle to the Romans* (London: Banner of Truth, 1958), 77–79.
123. Poole, *Annotations*, 3:483–484.
124. Thomas Chalmers, *Lectures on the Epistle to the Romans* (Edinburgh: Thomas Constable, 1848.), 1:90–117.
125. Charnock, *The Existence and Attributes of God*, 784.
126. Shedd, *Dogmatic Theology*, 1:432.
127. Berkhof, *Systematic Theology*, 446.
128. H. C. Hoeksema, "O.P.C. and the 'Free Offer'", 15th May 1973, *cf* Herman Hoeksema, *The Protestant Reformed Churches in America*, 339.
129. Calvin, *Matthew, Mark, and Luke*, 3:108.

and *"these times of ignorance God overlooked"* (Acts 17:30). He did not overlook their sin, but in His grace He bore with it, determining to delay the day of wrath.

His patience, like His other acts of goodness, is conducive to the wicked's repentance (Rom. 2:4; Acts 14:17, 17:27). "The heavens declare the gospel, not formally but fundamentally, in declaring the longsuffering of God, without which no gospel had been framed, or could have been expected. The heathen could not but read in those things favourable inclinations toward them."[130]

All these verses speak in terms of a dispensation of longsuffering. There are other verses that imply that such a dispensation exists, or has existed, when they speak of how God's manifestation of longsuffering will one day cease. This will definitely be so at the end of the age. But even during this age God starts to reveal His wrath against sin by showing less and less patience with some men, and with others, ceasing in His longsuffering and restraint of sin altogether, and hardening perverse unbelief (Prov. 1:24–33; Isa. 6:9–10; Jer. 16:13; Rom. 1:26,28; 1 Pet. 3:20). There comes a time, sometimes in this present age, when God's benevolence ceases once and for all toward the hardened sinner. God will *"love them no more"* (Hos. 9:15).

Herman Hoeksema says that Romans 1 speaks only of God's pursuing wrath, not of His restraining grace.[131] But how could God *"give them up"* (Rom. 1:26) unless He had first borne with them and restrained their sin? And why are they condemned for not being *"thankful"* (Rom. 1:21) if they reject evidence of what, Hoeksema claims, is wrath? Man should be thankful for mercy; but thankful for wrath? These men were *"storing up wrath"* (Rom. 2:5), because God in His patience was holding back from the wrath they deserved. The E.P.C.A. claim that a "longsuffering... referred to the non-elect" is a "longsuffering to no purpose".[132] But Romans 9:22 clearly refers longsuffering to the reprobate.

The revelation of God, especially in the gospel, is another

---

130. Charnock, *The Existence and Attributes of God*, 783.

131. Hoeksema, *The Protestant Reformed Churches in America*, 373; H. C. Hoeksema, "O.P.C. and the 'Free Offer'", 1st May 1974.

132. Rodman, *Universalism and the Reformed Churches*, 13.

Revelation of God and the Offer of the Gospel

evidence of God's sovereign benevolence towards men, and by these means He pursues the communication of His own nature to them.

From the beginning of time He has done this through natural revelation (Psa. 19:1–4 *cf* Rom. 10:16–18) which He hid from no man. Therefore none can plead that God has not graciously revealed Himself (Rom. 1:20), even though man has forfeited any right to such revelation since the fall. Men should be *"thankful"* (Rom. 1:21) for such mercies. It is not God's fault that they do not see Him, but the fault of their own perverse hearts (Rom. 1:21–23). Despite this, all of creation and all of God's provision for them (Acts 14:17, Acts 17:26*f*) are means intrinsically useful for communicating God's nature, and He places these means at their disposal.

It is foolish then to assert that the highest and plainest revelation of God in the law and the gospel is not also grace. The proclamation of the law and the gospel is a manifestation of a principle in God of sovereign love whereby He delights to reveal Himself to man and show Himself gracious and ready to forgive. As to when, and where, and how great, each manifestation shall be, God is perfectly free to express Himself.

To some He does not even send the gospel (Acts 16:7), or give an outward call in the preaching (Matt. 13:10–15). To others He sends the gospel. This is the grace of God's mercy, even if they do not receive it (Luke 10:13).[133] If it were not grace, how is it Chorazin was more inexcusable than Tyre (Matt. 11:20–22)?

Hoeksema will cry "What grace does the reprobate receive in the preaching?"[134] But I always thought grace depended on the Giver, not the receiver; on the intrinsic usefulness of the gift, not the use (or abuse) to which the gift is put. Does not Paul say this in Romans 3:1–2? *"What advantage then has the Jew?... Much in every way!*

133. Canons of Dort 1.3 "That men may be brought to believe, **God mercifully sends the messengers** of these most joyful tidings to whom He will and at what time He pleases; by whose ministry men are called to repentance and faith in Christ crucified."

134. Engelsma, "'Hyper-Calvinism' and the Call of the Gospel", 1st October 1974.

Chiefly, because to them were committed the oracles of God". Verse 3 is Hoeksema's objection: *"What if some did not believe?"* "What is their advantage?" Paul's reply is that God's faithfulness in giving is not to be judged by their faithlessness in receiving.

To yet others God will add to the grace of revelation, the grace of regeneration (Matt. 11:25). This was so in the case of Nineveh, to whom God sent not only the grace of revelation, but also the grace of repentance. When Jonah objects, God replies that he is rebelling not just against his commission from the Lord, but against God's very nature: *"I fled previously to Tarshish; for I know that You are a gracious and merciful God, slow to anger and abundant in lovingkindness"* (Jonah 4:2, *cf* v.11).

This principle of God's nature, expressed in the sending of the gospel to Nineveh, is described by Calvin who says: "Though indeed the Ninevites were alienated from God, yet as they were men, God, as He is the Father of the whole human race, acknowledged them as His own, at least to such an extent as to give them the common light of day, and other blessings of earthly life."[135]

The preaching of the gospel is a free manifestation of God's compassion—a principle whereby He pities man's condition and provides the outward means of salvation. God's nature of compassion is not an act of grace, but the expression of it in sending the gospel is.

Hulse speaks of God's **nature** as if it were an **act** of grace. "Common grace finds its highest expression in that desire and will of God, not only for fallen man's temporal well-being but for his soul's salvation and eternal happiness".[136] But God's "desire" (or better His "delight") refers to God's nature. That God delights that man would turn and be saved is not an act of grace, but a fact of His nature. It is therefore absurd to speak of common grace expressing itself in God's nature. God's nature expresses itself in acts of common grace.

God's nature is not an act of grace, but the revelation of His nature is. Stephen Charnock puts it: "The whole design of Scripture is to publish God's willingness to impart the fruits of the death

135. Calvin, *Twelve Minor Prophets*, 3:142.

136. Hulse, *The Free Offer*, 8.

of Christ."[137] That God should offer salvation to those that do not deserve it, and that He should reveal His delight that men turn to Him as a further inducement, is due only to His kindness and grace.

The preservation of society has been a traditional focus in discussing common grace. In this connection God's grace is manifested in the preservation and progress of culture, the restraint of sin in society, maintenance of law and order, the preservation of truth, and the performance of "civic" good.

Preservation of Society

This is an aspect of God's grace that relates to culture, independent of any goal of special grace. The focus is on the preservation or conservation of man as a species or community and therefore has little to do with common grace as the manifestation of God's kindness to individual sinners pursuing their individual well-being.

I do not intend to delve into this aspect of common grace as it is properly the subject for a separate book.

137. Stephen Charnock, *The Works of the Late Stephen Charnock* (London: Baynes, 1815), 6:545 as quoted Hulse, *The Free Offer*, 18.

Chapter Three

THE FREE OFFER OF CHRIST IN THE GOSPEL

The third question that arises from Engelsma's summing up is: Does God offer Christ and salvation to everyone in the preaching of the gospel?

There are in fact four questions that need to be answered:

- What is offered in the gospel?
- What is God's warrant for making the offer?
- What is our warrant for preaching the gospel?
- What is the sinner's warrant for believing?

Unfortunately these questions have not always been distinguished from each other as we shall see. Once again, we begin with a historical survey:

1. Historical Survey

John Calvin

Calvin vigorously opposed any restriction upon the preaching of the gospel. Sometimes he will refer to preaching as an "invitation to" or "demand for" conversion.[1] By such invitations "the grace of God is offered to us"[2] and the ungodly are therefore wholly inexcusable when "they ungratefully reject the offer which is made to them".[3]

He refers to the "free offer of salvation" in this dispensation which is a "time of benevolence". He says: "It displeases God, that the grace that He offers to us should be received by us with coolness

1. Calvin, *Eternal Predestination*, 106.
2. John Calvin, "The True Method of Giving Peace, and of Reforming the Church", *Tracts*, translated by Henry Beveridge (Edinburgh: Calvin Translation Society, 1851), 3:253–254.
3. Calvin, *Institutes*, 3.24.17.

and indifference". He continues: "While the gospel is preached to us, we know assuredly that the way is opened up for us into the kingdom of God, and that there is a signal of divine benevolence raised aloft, to invite us to receive salvation, for the opportunity of obtaining it must be judged of by the call. Unless, however we embrace this opportunity, we must fear the threatening that Paul brings forward—that in a short time, the door will be shut against all that have not entered in, while opportunity was afforded".[4]

But how can God make universal "offers" and "promises" when He does not intend to save all?

First Calvin points out that preaching itself is never universal. God commands the gospel be preached in all the world, but He still determines to what nations it will or will not go. Yet no one sees this as being inconsistent with the universality of the command. So too, wherever the gospel is preached God will have promiscuous offers made, but He will still determine to whom the Word is effective and who will remain in their ignorance.[5]

Secondly, all "promises" and "offers" made, however universal they be, always have a universal condition attached. "The promises are effectual only when we receive them in faith, but, on the contrary, when faith is made void, the promise is of no effect... All that is meant by the promise is, just that His mercy is offered to all who desire and implore it, and this none do save those whom He has enlightened."[6] "The doctrine of salvation... is abused when it is represented as effectually available to all."[7]

Thirdly, there is no inconsistency in God since it is not His fault that the reprobate receive not the word. "Though their perdition depends on the predestination of God, the cause and matter of it is in themselves."[8] But if you object, saying could not God "change the will of the wicked into good because He is omnipotent?", Calvin replies: "Clearly He could. Why then does He not do it? Because

4. Calvin, *Commentary Upon the Epistles of Paul the Apostle to the Corinthians* (Edinburgh: Calvin Translation Society, 1849), 2:247 *cf* 2:239–241.
5. Calvin, *Institutes*, 3.22.10.
6. Calvin, *Institutes*, 3.24.17.
7. Calvin, *Institutes*, 3.22.10.
8. Calvin, *Institutes*, 3.23.8.

He is unwilling. Why He is unwilling remains within Himself."[9]

Fourthly, however anthropomorphically we understand God's "wish that all should be saved", "the promiscuous call to salvation" is to be understood as its expression.[10]

Therefore God is not chargeable with insincerity or duplicity in making an offer to all.

Why does God make a universal call?

First to reach the elect, whose "consciences... may rest the more secure when they understand that there is no difference between sinners provided they have faith".[11]

Secondly, for the reprobate too there is an ultimate purpose in the plan of God—to leave them completely without excuse so that they "may not be able to allege that they have not an asylum to which they may betake themselves from the bondage of sin, while they ungratefully reject the offer which is made to them."[12]

The mixture of elect and reprobate is no reason for an omnipotent God to make an offer to all. But it is a reason for ignorant man. "We know not who belongs to the number of the predestinated, or does not belong; [therefore] our desire ought to be that all may be saved; and hence every person we meet, we will desire to be with us a partaker of peace. To God it will belong to make it available to those whom He has foreknown and predestinated."[13]

The Synod of Dort

The Synod of Dort upheld the free offer of the gospel stating that: "The promise of the gospel is that whosoever believes in Christ crucified shall not perish but have eternal life. This promise together with the command to repent and believe, ought to be declared and published to all nations, and to all persons promiscuously and without distinction, to whom God out of His good pleasure sends the gospel"[14] H. C. Hoeksema objects that this is not an "offer" but a "promise".[15] This is

9. Calvin, *Institutes*, 3.24.13 quoting Augustine.
10. Calvin, *Ezekiel*, 2:261–267.
11. Calvin, *Institutes*, 3.24.17.
12. Calvin, *Institutes*, 3.24.17.
13. Calvin, *Institutes*, 3.23.14 quoting Augustine.
14. Canons of Dort 2.5.
15. H. C. Hoeksema, "O.P.C. and the 'Free Offer'", 1st January 1974.

purely semantics. If one promises another eternal life on condition that he believes, he is making him an offer. Call it proposal, overture, tender or offer, this doesn't change the meaning.

The Canons also affirm the sincerity of God's offer. "As many as are called by the gospel are unfeignedly called (Lat. *serio vocantur*). For God has most earnestly and truly (Lat. *serio et verissime*) declared in His Word what is acceptable to Him, namely that those who are called should come unto Him. He also seriously (Lat. *serio*) promises rest of soul and eternal life to all who come to Him and believe."[16] Again Hoeksema objects that the question of God's sincerity is not involved since a "call" is not the same as an "offer" or "invitation". He translates *"serio"* as "seriously" throughout this article—as if it were saying simply that the call is a serious business.[17] *"Serio"* however carries more force than this and means "in earnest," "in all sincerity".[18]

Of course as soon as it is admitted that preaching is an invitation or offer to receive salvation through faith the question of God's sincerity naturally arises. This was voiced in the "opinions" of the Remonstrants who, like Hoeksema, could not reconcile the sincerity of the free offer and particular atonement.[19] Dort replied by rejecting neither and affirming both.

Engelsma however is at pains to sidestep such problems, even slavishly avoiding the implication of an invitation in interpreting Matthew 22:1–14. He presents a picture of God who "commands men to come to the feast of salvation prepared through Jesus' death and resurrection."[20] But the king in Matthew 22 did not command men to come to the wedding feast; he invited or called (καλεω) them. The reason those called by the king were so severely

16. Canons of Dort 3 & 4.8.
17. H. C. Hoeksema, "O.P.C. and the 'Free Offer'", 15th December 1973.
18. Refer to Charles T. Lewis and Charles Short, *A Latin Dictionary* (London: Harper & Brothers, 1890): "in earnest, seriously, in all sincerity".
19. *Opinions of the Remonstrants* (1618), 3.8 as provided in DeJong, *Crisis in the Reformed Churches*, 220ff: "Whomever God calls to salvation, he calls seriously, that is, with a sincere and completely unhypocritical intention and will to save; nor do we assent to the opinion of those who hold that God calls certain ones externally whom He does not will to call internally, that is, as truly converted, even before the grace of calling has been rejected."
20. Engelsma, "'Hyper-Calvinism' and the Call of the Gospel", 1st June 1974.

punished was not merely because they didn't come to the feast, but because they abused the gracious invitation they were given. Engelsma does not explain how God can be sincere in inviting (or calling) someone to a feast at which no place has been set for him or prepared through Jesus' death.

That God can be "unfeigned" in His call is explained: "It is not the fault of the gospel, nor of Christ offered therein, nor of God, who calls men by the gospel and confers upon them various gifts, that those who are called by the ministry of the Word refuse to come and be converted. The fault lies in themselves".[21]

The preaching of the gospel is "mercy" to all who hear. "God mercifully (Lat. *clementer*) sends the messengers of these most joyful tidings to whom He will and at what time He pleases; by whose ministry men are called to repentance and faith in Christ crucified."[22]

For the divines of Dort, sincerity depended on the Giver, not the receiver.

Westminster Confession

The Westminster Confession teaches that preaching consists in, not only a call to repentance and faith,[23] but also a proclamation that God "freely offers unto sinners life and salvation by Jesus Christ".[24] In the *Sum of Saving Knowledge* the divines stated: "In the word of God preached by sent messengers, the Lord makes offer of grace **to all sinners**, upon condition of faith in Jesus Christ."[25] Further: "This general offer in substance is equivalent to a special offer made to everyone in particular, Acts 16:31."[26]

But to offer man salvation through faith is not to tell him that Christ died personally for him. We may offer the "forgiveness of sins" to all (Acts 13:38), but this does not mean that forgiveness of sins has been purchased for all. It does not mean that atonement has been made for the sins of all.

21. Canons of Dort 3 & 4.9.
22. Canons of Dort 1.3.
23. WCF 15.1.
24. WCF 7.3. See also WLC Q. 67, WSC Q. 31.
25. The Sum of Saving Knowledge 3.
26. The Practical Use of Saving Knowledge 4.

To extend Archbishop Ussher's example[27] some imagine that God is like a wealthy sovereign with infinite treasure who offers of it to all, even though he only gives to some added inducement to overcome a perverse distrust which is the natural bent of his subjects.

But the Scriptures and Confession show that, even before offering, God has in mind those whom He will induce to come and has already put aside the treasure of forgiveness for those and those only. Forgiveness is indeed offered to all, but it has not been put aside for all. Hence forgiveness is not reserved for each and every man, but only for each and everyone that comes.

"Neither are any other redeemed by Christ, effectually called, justified, adopted, sanctified, and saved, but the elect only."[28]

Some maintain that the Confession, here, does not teach a particular atonement (i.e. purchasing definite benefits for the elect alone), but only a definite application of the (general) benefits of the atonement. They say that "redeemed" refers, not to the work of Christ in the atonement itself, but to the work of Christ through the Spirit applying its benefits (i.e. it is in apposition with "called, justified, adopted" etc). But Cunningham[29] points out that, in the 17th century, "redemption" was used to describe the purchase, not the application, of salvation.

The Confession[30] and Larger Catechism[31] both teach, not only a particular application, but also a particular "purchase" of "redemption", "reconciliation" and "everlasting inheritance" for the elect only. Hence the atonement itself was particular, and the treasure of salvation is available only to those who come. And the reason we are able to make such an offer is because atonement is available for any that believe (John 3:16).[32]

The Confession also maintains that the elect are not rich at the time God sets aside their treasure but only when the treasure is

27. MacGregor, "The Free Offer in the Westminster Confession", 56.
28. WCF 3.6.
29. Cunningham, *Historical Theology* 3:328.
30. WCF 8.5,8.
31. WLC Q. 59.
32. The Practical Use of Saving Knowledge 4.

actually given to them.[33]

Thus the divines of Westminster carefully avoided teaching an indefinite atonement on the one hand and eternal justification on the other.

The Savoy Declaration and the Baptist Confession of 1689

It is significant that the Congregationalists and Baptists made only one major change to the Westminster Confession (apart from those peculiar to Congregationalism and/or Baptism) and that was the addition of chapter 20: "Of the Gospel and of the Extent of the Grace Thereof".

This brief statement of the 17th century is not sufficient to defend the gospel against present day perversion and impoverishment, but it does show that, even then, men were realising the need for a definition of the gospel and the extent of grace.

John Owen

The only limit that John Owen places upon the offer is to restrict it to those who hear the preaching.[34] Apart from this, wherever the gospel is preached "proffers and tenders" are to be made "in the name of God to all".[35] The ultimate sin is for unbelievers to reject such tenders. "God who hath no need of them, nor their obedience or friendship, tenders them a treaty upon terms of peace. What greater condescension, love or grace could be conceived or desired?"[36] "Grace is so tendered in the preaching of the gospel, that none go without it, none are destitute of its aids, and assistance but those alone who, by a free act of their own wills do refuse and reject it."[37]

Owen means more than just a bare command to repent and believe when he speaks of a "proffer and tender". The "substance of the gospel" is "he that believeth shall be saved".[38] To all therefore we announce "*first,* What they ought to do, if they will do that which is acceptable to God; *secondly,* The sufficiency of salvation that is in Jesus Christ to all that believe in Him; *thirdly,* The

33. WCF 11.4.
34. Owen, *The Death of Death*, 200.
35. Owen, *The Death of Death*, 188.
36. Hulse, *The Free Offer*, 15.
37. Owen, "The Strength of Faith", cited by Shedd, *Dogmatic Theology*, 3:423.
38. Owen, *The Death of Death*, 199.

certain, infallible, inviolable connection that is between faith and salvation, so that whoever performs the one shall surely enjoy the other."[39] Any benefit of life promised must always be connected to a duty of faith.[40]

In preaching the gospel Owen would have us preach first, the depravity of man and his need of salvation; secondly, the duty of all to believe that there is salvation to be had in Christ; thirdly that the historical Jesus is this Saviour. And if a man has comprehended this much we may then proceed to entreat the sinner to trust in Christ as an all-sufficient Saviour. When the sinner shows signs of conversion we will press upon him the efficacy of Christ's atonement for him in particular.[41]

As to how God can be sincere in His offer to all, and yet save only some, Owen gives no answer. Such quibblings are of no consequence to the believer who trusts in the faithfulness of God. And to the hesitant soul it is a mere red herring: "Is it not time for you to leave disputing and questioning the sincerity and faithfulness of God in all these engagements?"[42]

As to the reason why God offers the gospel to all Owen answers that God thereby obtains the elect, "while the rest are hardened".[43]

What is our warrant for preaching the gospel to all? "A minister is not to make enquiry after... those secrets of the eternal mind of God... It is enough for them to search His revealed will, and thence to take their directions, from whence they have their commissions."[44]

Upon what basis do we offer salvation to all? Is it there for all? It is there for all that believe and this is sufficient.[45] We are not offering what cannot be given to those who come. "If there were a thousand worlds, the gospel of Christ might, upon this ground, be preached to them all, there being enough in Christ for the salvation of them all, if so be they will derive virtue from Him by touching

39. Owen, *The Death of Death*, 189.
40. Owen, *The Death of Death*, 201.
41. Owen, *The Death of Death*, 202.
42. Owen, "The Strength of Faith", 52.
43. Owen, *The Death of Death*, 201.
44. Owen, *The Death of Death*, 188.
45. Owen, *The Death of Death*, 201,271.

Him in faith". We do not call upon men to believe that Christ died for them. We call upon them to receive a salvation that is sufficient for their needs.[46]

Why do we preach to all men? First, because we are commanded to; secondly, because we do not know elect from reprobate; thirdly because we are bound to seek the good of all men; fourthly, because we are bound "to hope and judge well of all, even as it is meet for them". Therefore we "may make a proffer of Jesus Christ, with life and salvation in Him, notwithstanding that the Lord hath given His Son only to His elect".[47] We are therefore "bound to admonish all, and warn all men, to whom [we] are sent; giving the same commands, proposing the same promises, and making tenders of Jesus Christ in the same manner."[48]

What warrant does the sinner have to believe? Not that Christ has died for him particularly; but rather that it is his duty to believe (Matt. 11:28; Isa. 55:1), it is the command of God (1 John 3:23), life is promised to the believer (John 3:36), there is a threat for unbelief (John 3:36), Christ's blood is all-sufficient for believers (Acts 20:21; Eph. 5:2) and believers may be assured of salvation (Mark 16:16).[49]

Other Puritan Preaching

John Flavel preaches "Consider the nature, weight and worth of the mercies which are this day freely offered you... Christ the first born of mercies, and in Him pardon, peace and eternal salvation are set before you". Flavel depicts God in deadly earnest making such an offer: "His patience groans under the burden of your daily provocations; He loses nothing if you be damned, and receives no benefit if you be saved; yet the first motions of mercy and salvation to you freely arise out of His grace and good pleasure. God intreats you to be reconciled (2 Cor. 5:20). The blessed Lord Jesus, whose blood thy sins have shed, now freely offers that blood for thy reconciliation, justification and salvation, if thou wilt but sincerely accept Him ere it be too late... This may be the last overture of grace that ever God will make to your souls. Certainly there is an offer that will be

46. Owen, *The Death of Death*, 185.
47. Owen, *The Death of Death*, 186,188.
48. Owen, *The Death of Death*, 201, *cf* 188,202
49. Owen, *The Death of Death*, 298.

the last offer, a striving of the Spirit which will be His last striving; and after that no more offers."[50] Flavel entreated men with Christ's earnest suit to gain the hearts of sinners, His pathetical invitations, His fears and sorrows for the obstinacy of unbelievers and His offer of grace to every particular person.[51]

Thomas Manton suggests three reasons why we should believe God is "serious and in good earnest in these offers". We should consider first, God's entreaties; second that "it suiteth more with His delight that you should take hold of these offers and not refuse them"; third, God's grief that "men, through their own folly, neglect that which should do them good".[52]

Thomas Brooks spoke of "Christ [showing] His free grace and His condescending love by [inviting] the very worst of sinners to open to Him."[53]

Anthony Burgess describes the external call as "consisting in the tender and offer of grace, inviting of men to come in."[54]

Obadiah Sedgwick describes the plight of the reprobate on judgment day: "I was offered Christ and grace. I felt Him knocking by His Spirit; but I slighted Him, grieved Him, and rejected Him."[55]

David Dickson protests that the "means of execution of [the] decrees" is not the cause of the "stumbling of any man". But "the offer of grace and declaration of God's goodness is so laid out in common, that whosoever doth not embrace the same, is made inexcusable."[56]

Amyraldianism

In the first two chapters of this book we have discussed two basic principles of God's nature. The first is that whereby He delights that men would turn to Him; the second is that whereby He delights in sovereign love. God expresses both of these in His dealings with men generally.

50. John Flavel, "Sermon 1 on Rev. 3:20" *Works of John Flavel*. Vol. IV. (London: Banner of Truth, 1968), 26*f.*
51. Hulse, *The Free Offer*, 14–15.
52. Hulse, *The Free Offer*, 15.
53. Hulse, *The Free Offer*, 17.
54. Hulse, *The Free Offer*, 16.
55. Hulse, *The Free Offer*, 16.
56. Hulse, *The Free Offer*, 16.

Because He delights in sovereign love He manifests sovereign benevolence which includes provision of the means intrinsically useful for finding salvation.

But these principles in God were not the sole sufficient cause for Him to make atonement for men. While God certainly expresses these principles of His nature in making atonement, yet the ultimate motive for such an act on behalf of some lies hidden in Himself along with the reason why He determined in eternity to choose and love intensely His elect. The motive behind the atonement and the motive behind election cannot be separated.

Unfortunately Amyraut thought they could. Amyraut taught that "the motive impelling God to redeem men was benevolence, or love to men in general".[57] He therefore sent Christ into the world to die for all men. This proposition is Arminianism. On this basis God offers salvation to all. Atonement is literally available for all.

However God knew that all men have a "moral inability" to believe. He therefore "determined to give His efficacious grace to a certain number of the human race and thus secure their salvation".[58] This proposition is basically Calvinism.

Amyraut taught that, in making the atonement, God has an "absolute intention" for the elect, and a "conditional intention" for the reprobate in case they do believe. This of course is nonsense. God cannot intend what He will not purpose. He may "delight in" what He yet does not purpose. He may pursue it. But He cannot intend it and not obtain, without violence being done to His omnipotence. What God intended by the atonement He certainly achieved. Universal redemption is an untenable position. Berkhof points out that the followers of this school were not able to hold Arminianism and Calvinism in such tension and eventually drifted to one camp or the other.[59]

The French National Synod of 1637 dismissed Amyraut with a mild censure, and prohibited such expressions of his as "conditional decrees", "Christ died equally for all", "God's velleity,

57. Hodge, *Systematic Theology*, 2:222.
58. Hodge, *Systematic Theology*, 2:222.
59. Louis Berkhof, *The History of Christian Doctrine* (London: Banner of Truth, 1968), 190.

or vehement desire of things that do not come to pass".[60] Amyraut was allowed to return to his post as teacher in the theological school of Saumur.

Amyraut must share the blame for this extraordinary decision. He had unswervingly sworn allegiance to the Canons of Dort. He was either dull or dishonest. But the Synod itself can hardly be exonerated for its action in restoring Amyraut to his post as teacher. It is obvious that compromise was the spirit of the day as the church sought to close ranks in the face of a fresh onslaught of persecution.[61]

John Davenant taught along similar lines in England. He, along with three others, was chosen by James I to represent the Church of England at the international Synod of Dort. Though he was not part of the Westminster Assembly, a few who sympathised with his views were, notably Edmund Calamy. Whatever influence these men had on the two assemblies, neither Dort nor Westminster adopted Amyraldian views.

Rodman claims that the "desire" theology of Murray and Stonehouse is no more than Amyraldianism in which "intention" is replaced by "desire".[62] To be fair, Murray and Stonehouse will have nothing to do with a *decretum universale hypotheticum,* which is the pivot on which Amyraldianism turns. Nonetheless Rodman insists that both schemes are "creatures that belong to the same family".[63] It must be admitted that Murray and Stonehouse do not sufficiently guard against making God's general benevolence the source of the atonement.

Formula Consensus Helvetica

The Swiss churches, alarmed at the French toleration of Amyraldianism drew up the *Formula Consensus Helvetica* ("Form of Agreement of the

60. Roger Nicole, "Amyraldianism" *Encyclopaedia of Christianity.* Edited by Edwin Hartshorn Palmer (Marshallton: The National Foundation for Christian Education, 1964) 1:187.
61. The Reformed Church of France is not alone. Many Presbyterian Churches now read the Westminster Confession in the light of a Declaratory Act, which is Amyraldian, and hence contradicts the very Reformed Confession it is supposed to be shedding light upon.
62. Rodman, *Universalism and the Reformed Churches*, 11.
63. Rodman, *Universalism and the Reformed Churches*, 11.

Helvetic Churches") under the direction of Heidegger, Turretin, and Gernler. This Confession, which is infralapsarian,[64] affirms that the source of the atonement is in God's special love towards His elect,[65] not in general love toward mankind.[66]

It upholds the doctrine of God's witness to Himself in nature and providence, and His longsuffering in history. Men are thereby left without excuse since they are not thankful for these blessings.[67]

God's call is both "earnest and sincere". The gospel accomplishes the salvation of the elect, or demonstrates the "inexcusableness of the rest". This call is "universally proffered".[68] God's special grace need not be universal for the call to be "serious and true", or for God to be "candid and sincere".[69]

The Marrow Controversy

One of the most interesting controversies to afflict Reformed churches was the "Marrow" Controversy in the Church of Scotland in the early 18th century. I say "interesting", not just because of the doctrinal issues that were the focus (Amyraldianism, Antinomianism, Neonomianism), but even more (to my mind, at least) because it illustrates how controversies in the church arise and often get out of hand. So if I appear to digress here it is because of the lessons to be learnt about controversy which (to my mind at least) are of even more benefit than the controversy itself.

The back story was a book written in the previous century by Edward Fisher: *The Marrow of Modern Divinity*. In it, he purports to be finding a middle ground between legalism on the one hand, and antinomianism on the other. Fisher's credentials in this respect were not impeccable. Chad Van Dixhoorn, a leading researcher of the Westminster Assembly and of that period, states that Fisher was "well connected to the antinomian underground"[70]

64. Formula Consensus Helvetica 4.
65. FCH 5.
66. FCH 6.
67. FCH 18.
68. FCH 19.
69. FCH 20.
70. Chad Van Dixhoorn, "The Strange Silence of Prolocutor Twisse: Predestination and Politics in the Westminster Assembly's Debate over Justification" *Electronic Sixteenth Century Journal* 63, no. 2 (June 2009):.415.

and "appears to have tailored his work to avoid [the] censure" of the Westminster Assembly's committee dedicated to finding and questioning suspected antinomians.[71] John Trapp labelled him a "sly antinomian."[72]

Of more concern (at least, in relation to the "Free Offer") was Fisher's espousal of Amyraut's "hypothetical universalism" (HU). This has been disputed by some, though a number of others have noted it. Dr Thomas M'Crie (1772–1835), in a recommendatory preface to Owen's *Death of Death,* wrote that he could "not reconcile [Owen] with the 'Marrow' doctrine... according to which the believer regards Christ as his, not in possession, but in the free offer of the Gospel."[73] More recently Mark Jones has noted that "many scholars try with all their might to avoid the implications of this thought, but I simply cannot see how we can deny that the *Marrow* teaches HU."[74]

In this regard Fisher certainly contributed to the confusion by his own loose terminology. For example, "Be verily persuaded in your heart that Jesus Christ is yours, and that you shall have life and salvation by him; that whatsoever Christ did for the redemption of mankind, he did it for you."[75] "God the Father, as he is in his Son Jesus Christ, moved with nothing but with his free love to mankind lost, hath made a deed of gift and grant unto them all."[76] There is more to this than simply whether "there is a universal call to all sinners to receive Christ with a promise (or offer) of mercy to all that do so" as Iain Murray claims.[77]

The following century this work became the focus of controversy in the Church of Scotland. The spark that lit the powder keg was a

71. Van Dixhoorn, "The Strange Silence of Prolocutor Twisse", 416.
72. David R. Como, *Blown by the Spirit: Puritanism and the Emergence of an Antinomian Underground in Pre-Civil-War England* (Stanford: Stanford University Press 2004), 4.
73. John Macleod, *Scottish Theology: in Relation to Church History* (London: Banner of Truth, 1974), 161.
74. Mark Jones, "The Marrow: Some Questions", *Reformation 21*, 14 January 2016, https://www.reformation21.org/blogs/the-marrow-part-1.php
75. Edward Fisher, *The Marrow of Modern Divinity*, 2.3.2, Kindle.
76. Fisher, *Marrow of Modern Divinity*, 2.3.3.
77. Iain Murray, "The Free Offer of the Gospel" *Banner of Truth Magazine* (July 1958): 8.

simple question put to a ministerial candidate in the Presbytery of Auchterarder: "Do you agree that it is not sound and orthodox to teach that we forsake sin in order to our coming to Christ, and instating us in covenant with God?" This was known as the "Auchterarder Creed."

At first this seems like a no-brainer: obviously we are to forsake sin in coming to Christ. The call to "repent" everywhere accompanies the call to "believe": Jesus taught this (Mark 1:14–15), Peter taught it (Acts 2:38), Paul taught it (Acts 20:18–20), John taught it (1 John 3:5–6). Also, the Auchterarder Creed appears to contradict the Church's own Westminster Confession which teaches that: "although repentance be not to be rested in as any satisfaction for sin", yet "it is of <u>such necessity to all sinners</u>, that none may expect pardon without it."[78]

But (and here was the problem), it was a trick question. The "right" answer the Presbytery was looking for was that "it is not sound and orthodox to teach that we <u>[*have the ability, in ourselves, without the Spirit, to*]</u> forsake sin in order to our coming to Christ." Though even today, those who defend the "creed" cannot agree on what the Presbytery was getting at: some claim they were seeking to guard against Neonomianism (i.e. seeing repentance as a "good work" that helps "merit" salvation); others that it was to guard against hyper-Calvinism (i.e. since salvation is all of grace you shouldn't offer salvation till someone evidences the grace of repentance).

Many Evangelicals in the Church of Scotland at the time supported the use of the "creed", though John Macleod queries their wisdom in this, as well as expressing concern over other aspects of their cause. He comments: "It is but fair to bear in mind that the Evangelicals sometimes gave a handle to their opponents by the incautious way in which they expressed themselves."[79] Many defenders of the "creed" today also acknowledge it was "poorly worded".

The candidate at the time at first agreed; then disagreed (with the plain meaning); then was disbarred. The Assembly of the Church

78. WCF 15.3.

79. John Macleod, *Scottish Theology*, 156.

of Scotland took up his case and condemned the Presbytery. Lines were drawn. Sides were taken. The fight was on.

Those opposed to the Assembly accused that body of legalism, since (it seemed to them) the Church was teaching a form of salvation by works (i.e. the "work" of repentance). The Assembly in turn accused their opponents of antinomianism, since (it seemed to them) they denied the necessity of repentance.

The opponents of the Assembly then produced Fisher's *Marrow of Modern Divinity,* as proof against the place of any works in salvation. The Church saw this as further proof of their antinomianism and placed it on its own index of banned books. Predictably, many then went out and bought it. In the end, some of the "Marrow Men" (as they were termed) separated (though over a different issue: that of patronage), and formed the Associate Presbytery.

Traditionally, evangelicals have sided with the Marrow Men. This, for two reasons:

1. The Church of Scotland at the time had lost a lot of the evangelical fervour it had demonstrated in the previous century. Moderatism was beginning to appear. At the same time, a professor charged with heresy was let off lightly. All this does not sit well with evangelicals.
2. On the other hand, the Marrow Men were obviously sincere and zealous for the gospel of Christ—men like Thomas Boston, and Ralph and Ebenezer Erskine. Our sympathies are with them.

But, as the saying goes: "The enemy of my enemy is my friend." This may have led the Marrow Men to be too quick to resort to *The Marrow.* The Marrow Men were mostly orthodox in their beliefs. Far from embracing antinomianism, Boston, Erskine and the others insisted on the necessity of good works.

Nor did the Marrow Men hold to "hypothetical universalism." But they were not always clear in the way they expressed themselves. "According to them all sinners are legatees under Christ's testament, not indeed in the essence but *in the administration* of the covenant of grace, but the testament becomes effectual only in the case of the elect."[80] Also sometimes they were rather too zealous in their defence of *The Marrow*, defending the indefensible. Boston's notes, when he reissued *The Marrow* spill more ink defending the book than was spilt in writing the original. And sometimes he seems to resort to special pleading in his defence.[81]

John Macleod comments: "In connection, too, with *The Marrow* itself, there were a good many unguarded expressions that, taken by themselves, had an Antinomian sound. These had to be explained and glossed when Boston came to edit the work in detail."[82]

This is a warning to us all: we are all prone to look for support wherever we can when involved in controversy. It is difficult enough to get to the bottom of church disputes, even today; let alone imagining we can unravel all the in's and out's of a bun fight as confusing as this, on the other side of the world, 300 years ago.

My heart is with Thomas Boston who sided with the Auchterarder party; I have benefited from some of his writings. But my sympathies are with the young ministerial candidate. I believe it is dangerous to preach a gospel that does not insist on the "necessity to all sinners" to repent before they "may expect pardon".

The Hyper-Calvinist Debate of 18th Century

This debate centred around the doctrine of total depravity, not particular atonement,[83] although Article 33 of the Gospel Standard churches cites "special redemption", as well as lack of "creature power", as a reason for not addressing the unconverted.[84]

The debate took root in the early 18th century in some English churches which would not even call men to faith and repentance, let alone offer salvation, unless they showed signs of conversion. Andrew Fuller's *The Gospel Worthy of all Acceptation* refutes this position.[85]

---

80. Berkhof, *Systematic Theology*, 398.
81. E.g. Boston, no less than nine times, takes pains to explain Fisher's ambiguous phraseology that in Christ there is "a deed of gift and grant to all."
82. John Macleod, *Scottish Theology*, 157.
83. Cunningham, *Historical Theology*, 2:344.
84. Bernard Honeysett, "The Ill-fated Articles" *Reformation Today* (Summer 1970): 26.
85. See T.E. Watson, "Andrew Fuller's Conflict with Hypercalvinism", *How Shall*

William Cunningham

William Cunningham rightly sees that the question of a warrant for the offer is two questions:

- What is our warrant?
- What is God's warrant?

"The neglect of keeping these two questions distinct, has sometimes introduced error and confusion into the discussion of this subject".[86] Cunningham also rightly points out that our only warrant is God's command. Nothing more, nothing less. On this basis we "hold out to them, in His name, pardon and acceptance, through the blood of the atonement".[87]

As to the question of God's warrant Cunningham provides no answer. To those who seek a solution in the "intrinsic sufficiency" of the atonement he says "this has manifestly nothing to do with the question".[88] He is satisfied that "we can find much that is fitted to show positively that God does not, in offering pardon and acceptance to men indiscriminately, act insincerely or deceptively".[89] He sees the problem as an extension of that between man's free agency and God's sovereignty.

John Bonar

John Bonar dealt with the free offer in a sermon on Proverbs 8:4,6, "The Universal Calls and Invitations of the Gospel Consistent with the Total Depravity of Man and Particular Redemption."[90]

He first lays down the grounds which are necessary before we may call all to salvation and before any may come. These are that a Saviour must be provided, and that salvation must be freely offered.[91] Bonar insists that a universal offer no more implies a universal atonement, than a universal command implies universal

They Hear?: a symposium of papers read at the Puritan and Reformed Studies Conference. Edited by Martyn Lloyd-Jones (London: Evangelical Magazine, 1960), 22–29.

86. Cunningham, *Historical Theology*, 2:345.
87. Cunningham, *Historical Theology*, 2:345.
88. Cunningham, *Historical Theology*, 2:348.
89. Cunningham, *Historical Theology*, 2:346.
90. John Bonar, "The Universal Calls and Invitations of the Gospel" *Banner of Truth Magazine* (February 1959): 11.
91. Bonar, "The Universal Calls and Invitations of the Gospel", 16.

ability.[92] He also makes the point that this is not Arminianism, nor anything like it, since the Arminian has no salvation to offer, but only salvability.[93]

But how can God be sincere in offering salvation to all when it is not there for all? To this objection he replies that only a person who comes to God for salvation and finds it not, can accuse God of deceit. "God neither mocks nor deceives anyone. Where there is no confidence placed, there can be no deceit experienced."[94]

What is our warrant to preach? "It is the command of God to offer Christ."[95] What is the sinner's warrant to believe? It is the invitation of God. "If your name is not in the invitation of the gospel, neither is it in the condemnation of the law."[96] What is preaching? It is telling men that "Christ is God's gift to mankind sinners". That "God calleth you by ten thousand expostulations and entreaties". That "Christ calleth you by His sufferings, by His death, by His tears of compassion, by His entreaties of grace."[97]

The words of preaching are themselves "drops of the compassion of God", whereby He "directly, personally, and earnestly beseeches us to be reconciled to Him—eternal life in offer, Christ in offer, everlasting blessedness in offer, and everyone either receiving or rejecting these offers."[98]

Robert M'Cheyne

Robert M'Cheyne also preached on Proverbs 8:4, "There is no subject more misunderstood by unconverted souls than the unconditional freeness of Christ. So little idea have we naturally of free grace, that we cannot believe that God can offer a Saviour to us, while we are in a wicked, hell-deserving condition".

Do you draw back fearing you are not elect? "To you I answer, nobody ever came to Christ because they knew themselves to be of the elect... Christ nowhere invites the elect to come to Him.

92. Bonar, "The Universal Calls and Invitations of the Gospel", 17.
93. Bonar, "The Universal Calls and Invitations of the Gospel", 19.
94. Bonar, "The Universal Calls and Invitations of the Gospel", 19.
95. Bonar, "The Universal Calls and Invitations of the Gospel", 20.
96. Bonar, "The Universal Calls and Invitations of the Gospel", 20.
97. Bonar, "The Universal Calls and Invitations of the Gospel", 20.
98. Bonar, "The Universal Calls and Invitations of the Gospel", 20–21.

The question for you is not, Am I one of the elect? But am I one of the human race?... Are you not a man?... then Christ is offered to you.... If you could die and say that Christ had never been offered to you, you would have an easier hell than you are like to have!"[99]

Charles Hodge

Charles Hodge bases the free offer on the nature of the atonement. This was essentially a penal atonement, not a pecuniary atonement. If it were pecuniary, anyone could pay the debt, and the debtor is automatically free. But in a court of law there is no automatic pecuniary release. The offender himself must pay for his crime. If a substitute is accepted it is not automatic but by the grace of the court. And the substitute's punishment must be of at least equal value to that which the original offender would have had meted out to him.[100]

Then Hodge appears to draw a distinction between the atonement and redemption (i.e. the application of the benefits purchased by the atonement). Although Christ had in mind His elect, and them alone, when He made atonement, yet His sacrifice can be abstracted from them. It is only when they are born again and justified that the benefits of the atonement accrue to them.[101] "The application of its benefits is determined by the covenant between the Father and the Son. Those for whom it was specially rendered are not justified from eternity... They are by nature children of wrath" and "remain in this state until they believe". This is because the atonement is penal, not pecuniary and therefore it is by the grace of the Court (Father and Son) that the benefits of a substitute accrue at all.

Hodge deduces that the benefits of the atonement are there to accrue to anyone that believes. We may therefore offer such an atonement to all. The fact that the Father, even in making the atonement determined to whom the benefits will accrue is neither here nor there.[102] A. A. Hodge holds a similar view.[103]

---

99. Andrew Bonar, *Memoir and Remains of R.M. M'Cheyne* (London: Banner of Truth, 1966), 365*ff.*
100. Hodge, *Systematic Theology*, 2:470*ff.*
101. Hodge, *Systematic Theology*, 2:470.
102. Hodge, *Systematic Theology*, 2:409.
103. A.A. Hodge, *Outlines of Theology* (London: Banner of Truth, 1972), 419.

The main objection to this view is that "it suggests that the active obedience of Christ may be imputed to, and the gifts of effectual calling, sanctification, and glorification bestowed upon us, a constituency different from that for whom God in Christ has provided 'a vicarious penalty to satisfy guilt.'"[104]

While we reject the doctrine of eternal justification[105], the atonement cannot be abstracted from those for whom it was made. When the Confession states "neither are any other redeemed by Christ"[106] it is speaking, not of the application of the atonement, but the atonement itself.[107] Therefore we conclude that Hodge's argument "has manifestly nothing to do with the question".

R. L. Dabney also distinguished between the atonement and its application. He also believed that Amyraldianism was a non-issue

R. L. Dabney

since there is no order of decrees in the mind of God.[108] But the issue with Amyraldianism is not so much with the order of the decrees but with God's intention in them.

Dabney argues for an indefinite application of John 3:16 saying that it refers to a "propension of benevolence [in God], not matured into a volition to redeem, of which Christ's mission is a sincere manifestation to all sinners."[109]

But here B. B. Warfield's comment on John 3:16 is pertinent, *viz*: "The 'world' that God so loved that He gave His Son for it,—surely that is not the 'world' that He loved so little as to leave it to take or leave the Son so given, as its own wayward heart might dictate; but the 'world' that He loved enough, after giving His Son for it, prevalently to move upon with His quickening Spirit and

104. Donald MacLeod, "Misunderstandings of Calvinism II", *Banner of Truth Magazine* (February 1968): 20.
105. WCF 11.4.
106. WCF 3.6.
107. Cunningham, *Historical Theology* 2:327.
108. Dabney, "God's Indiscriminate Proposals of Mercy", 305*ff.* Dabney is not entirely consistent: in Dabney, *Lectures in Systematic Theology*, 235,519, he condemns Amyraldianism since it cannot say that Christ purchased the grace of effectual calling for His people.
109. Dabney, "God's Indiscriminate Proposals of Mercy", 313.

graciously lead into offered salvation."[110]

W. G. T. Shedd fails to distinguish between what is God's warrant to offer and what is ours. He gives the following grounds for a universal offer.[111]

W. G. T. Shedd

1. The divine command (Mark 16:15).
2. The mixture of elect and reprobate in the world.
3. The sufficiency of the atonement. He distinguishes between atonement "sufficient for all" and redemption "efficient for the elect".[112] See note on Hodge.
4. God is not efficiently preventing the reprobate but encouraging him by common grace.
5. God desires every man to believe.
6. It is only the reprobate that prevents the atonement being applied to him.
7. The call of God to sinners is not to believe that Christ died for them in particular, but that He died for sinners.
8. "The preacher is to hope and expect from God the best and not the worst for every man".
9. Even the reprobate benefit from the atonement.

Some of these reasons appear to be more or less irrelevant. Shedd also offers three reasons why all men should have the gospel preached to them:

1. It is the duty of every man to trust in the atonement.
2. It is the most impressive mode of preaching the law.
3. It will reveal the obstinacy of man's will.

As already mentioned John Murray and Ned Stonehouse are far from clear when it comes to distinguishing between God's will

110. Warfield, "God's Immeasurable Love", 509. To be fair, it should be noted that Warfield himself veers away from this explanation by adding: "But it is difficult to feel they quite exhaust the meaning of the great words of the text."
111. Shedd, *Dogmatic Theology*, 2:455, 482.
112. Shedd, *Dogmatic Theology*, 2:468.

John Murray and Ned Stonehouse

and the source of that will which is His nature. I quote from their conclusion: "The full and free offer of the gospel is a grace bestowed upon all. Such grace is necessarily a manifestation of love or lovingkindness in the heart of God."[113] If this were qualified as in chapter two we could accept this.

But then this: "And this lovingkindness is revealed to be of a character or kind that is correspondent with the grace bestowed. The grace offered is nothing less than salvation in its richness and fullness. The love or lovingkindness that lies back of that offer is not anything less; it is the will to that salvation". Murray and Stonehouse have again confused God's nature with His will.

But apart from this they imply that the source of the atonement and the source of the offer to men in general is the same. It is certainly true that in making the offer God manifests a kindness that springs simply from His delight in sovereign love. But the atonement finds its source, not in the general kindness of God, but in God's eternal decree of election whereby He determined to seek invariably the good of the elect. God's immutable lovingkindness towards His elect is hardly of the same "character and kind" as His occasional benevolence toward all men.

Elsewhere Murray follows a different tack. He seeks to explain how "the atonement is that which laid the ground for the preaching of repentance to all nations".[114] He reasons that God's foreknowledge or special love for the elect was the source of the atonement since they are the ones that benefit. But lesser benefits also accrue to the reprobate in the gospel age. Therefore the source of the atonement must also have been a lesser love for them. "We may not exclude from that love of which the atonement is the provision this general love of God to lost mankind."[115]

We would do well to be wary of this position or of any other attempt to find the source of the atonement in God's general benevolence. It is true that, by God's grace and benevolence salvation is offered to all, but Scripture nowhere gives us reason to believe that God

---

113. Murray and Stonehouse, *The Free Offer of the Gospel*, 27
114. John Murray, "The Atonement and the Free Offer of the Gospel", 24.
115. John Murray, "The Atonement and the Free Offer of the Gospel", 33.

had anyone else in mind in making the atonement other than His own. Neither God's general love for mankind, nor a specific "lesser love" towards those living under the gospel, nor His abhorrence at the death of the sinner, can be considered a sufficient cause for the atonement.

Murray tries to maintain the distinction between God's benevolence towards men in general and His special love towards the elect, but when he meanders off on groundless theories based upon a wider bearing of the atonement, he only clouds the issue.

The idea of a wider bearing of the atonement is not new. Some, like the Marrow Men, expressed it in an atonement "sufficient for all, efficient to the elect"—a view espoused in various forms by Hodge, Strong, Dabney and Shedd. Others spoke of the universal benefits that accrue to men in general from the atonement.[116] But very few try and make this wider bearing the basis of a universal offer as do Shedd and Murray. After all, we are not offering a few side benefits to men in the gospel, but salvation itself.

Protestant Reformed Churches

The Protestant Reformed Church strongly denies any charge of Hyper-Calvinism.[117] Engelsma believes we do have a warrant for preaching, and that is the command of God. Sinners also have a warrant to believe, and that is that "God has perfected salvation in Jesus Christ". Therefore "we proclaim Christ crucified to them, presenting Christ in the preaching of His Word, always, of course as the righteousness of God. We pass upon them the judgment of the gospel, that they are by nature guilty and totally depraved, children of wrath, exposed to the damnation of hell except they repent. We call them in the name of God to repent and believe. As we command all men everywhere to repent we proclaim to all the promise that whosoever believeth in Christ crucified, shall not perish but have everlasting life."[118]

116. John Flavel, "Sermon 12 on Heb. 10:14" *Works of John Flavel* (London: Banner of Truth, 1968), 1:159.
117. David Engelsma, "Our Protestant Reformed Position Regarding the 'Free Offer of the Gospel'" *Standard Bearer*, 1st November 1973; Engelsma, "'Hypercalvinism' and the Call of the Gospel", 1st April 1974.
118. Engelsma, "Our Protestant Reformed Position Regarding the 'Free Offer of the Gospel'", 15th December 1973.

Of course there can be none of the Puritans' language, representing God "tendering or offering grace to all", or Christ making an "earnest suit to gain the hearts of sinners". This is anathema. H. C. Hoeksema reasons that "if Christ died and paid the price of redemption for the elect only, and for none other, then God has no salvation to offer the reprobate... Such an offer could not possibly be bonafide."[119] Engelsma also denies that God is gracious by way of any offer, or that there is any benevolence in God towards men in general, or that God "desires" to save everyone. These are the issues facing the Protestant Reformed Church in the debate.[120]

Engelsma believes in "lively preaching, including the serious call to repentance and faith".[121] He disclaims that in Protestant Reformed Church preaching there is any "lack of ardour to gain and save many", or "[unwillingness] to beseech others to be reconciled to God," or any "delight in preaching men to hell"[122]—a claim that could be verified if one were able to listen to their preaching.

But this is surely the biggest strain in Protestant Reformed Church theology. They are trying to be perfect, but not "as God is perfect". According to Engelsma God merely "commands men to come to the feast of salvation";[123] Engelsma beseeches them. God will no more than seriously call; Engelsma calls with an ardour to gain and save many. God apparently would have no delight in seeing the reprobate saved; Engelsma has no delight in seeing them go to hell.

By what right does Engelsma take to himself affections that he believes are contrary to God's nature? Or does he believe that holy humanity is "more generous and tender than God"?

119. H. C. Hoeksema, "O.P.C. and the 'Free Offer'", 15th September 1973.

120. Engelsma, "Our Protestant Reformed Position Regarding the 'Free Offer of the Gospel'", 1st November 1973.

121. Engelsma, "'Hypercalvinism' and the Call of the Gospel", 1st April 1974.

122. Engelsma, "'Hypercalvinism' and the Call of the Gospel", 1st October 1974.

123. Engelsma, "'Hypercalvinism' and the Call of the Gospel", 1st June 1974.

2. The Free Offer

a) What is Offered in the Gospel

The question is whether God in the gospel merely commands all men to repent and believe, or whether He earnestly and sincerely calls upon all men to receive salvation by repenting and believing.

There is ample evidence in Scripture to show that, in our preaching, we are not only to call men and women to repentance and faith, but we are to offer them salvation if they should do so. Our commission is not merely to preach repentance, but *"repentance and remission of sins"* (Luke 24:47). This was the message of the apostles.

Peter preached: *"Repent, and let every one of you be baptized in the name of Jesus Christ for the remission of sins; and you shall receive the gift of the Holy Spirit."* (Acts 2:38). Even when men had shown no sign of repenting he still proclaimed a salvation to be had if they would do so. *"Repent therefore and be converted, that your sins may be blotted out, so that times of refreshing may come from the presence of the Lord"* (Acts 3:19).

Paul's preaching contains the same message. His presentation of the gospel in Acts 13 is typical of Apostolic preaching. He begins by declaring to his listeners the God of history (Acts 13:17*ff*), who became part of our history in Jesus Christ (Acts 13:23*ff*). The pivot of history is the vindication of Christ by His death and resurrection (Acts 13:30*ff*). On this basis then Paul offers them forgiveness of sins (Acts 13:38) and justification if they will believe (Acts 13:39). He concludes with a terrible warning for unbelievers (Acts 13:41). This is pure preaching of the gospel, the whole of which is to be preached to the hardest of sinners.

In his preaching Paul presented Christ, not just as *"the righteousness of God"* but as the One who *"died for our sins according to the scriptures"*. This gospel of Christ is that *"by which also you are saved, if you hold fast that word which I preached to you—unless you believed in vain."* (1 Cor. 15:1–4).

Christ's invitations also offer salvation. He invites *"all you who labour and are heavy laden"* to come to Him and offers them *"rest for your souls"* (Matt. 11:28–30). He offers life to those that will believe (John 3:36), as well as warning unbelievers of the wrath of God.

God's invitations in the Old Testament are no less gracious. His command is to *"all you ends of the earth"* to *"look to Me".* Such is the duty every creature is obligated to perform simply because he is a creature. But God adds to His command an offer of salvation. *"Look to me, and be saved, you the ends of the earth"* (Isa. 45:22, *cf* 55:1–5).

Even as every created being is under obligation to look to God, so every fallen creature is duty-bound to repent and turn back to God. This is the duty of fallen man and fallen angel. But the gospel is more than just a call to duty to a rebellious creature. There is, after all, no gospel for the devil, even though he too is under obligation to repent and turn.[124]

The gospel is a gracious offer of salvation to man if he will perform his duty. There is no obligation upon God's part to make such an offer. Even when sinful man repents he is still an *"unprofitable servant"* (Luke 17:10). That God not only commands, but also holds out salvation is pure grace.

b) The Warrant for God's Offer

By this we mean how can God offer salvation to those for whom it was never purchased?

First it needs to be reasserted that sincerity depends upon the Giver, not the receiver. "Will anyone contend that God cannot sincerely offer salvation to a free moral agent unless in addition to the invitation He exerts a special influence which will induce the person to accept it."[125] God does not efficiently prevent the reprobate accepting the salvation offered. God clearly delights that he would accept it. He has also given ample evidence, through

124. Commenting on Col. 1:20 *"...by Him to reconcile all things to Himself, by Him, whether things on earth or things in heaven, having made peace through the blood of His cross"* Calvin notes that Christ did not make peace for "the devils", nor "even [for] wicked men"—though "there is a difference, inasmuch as the benefit of redemption is offered to the latter, but not to the former."

125. Loraine Boettner, *The Reformed Doctrine of Predestination* (Philadelphia: P&R 1968), 283.

His benevolence, that He is ready to pursue the well-being of His creatures, even the reprobate. These are no evidences of insincerity.

Secondly, God is not offering what is not available to anyone that will come to Him. And, after all, a charge of insincerity can only be sustained if it can be shown that someone has accepted God's offer only to find it void. But "if no one repents without finding God propitious, then this sentence is filled up."[126] This, Christ expresses when He says: *"All that the Father gives Me will come to Me,"* and *"the one who comes to Me I will by no means cast out"* (John 6:37).

The sufficiency of the atonement has often been made the ground of a universal offer. This should not be understood in the sense of "available to all but applied only to the elect". Nor is the intrinsic infinite value of the atonement of any consequence in this debate, as Cunningham points out. But that an atonement is provided, sufficient to meet the needs of each and any that will come, is certainly a necessary ground for the offer.

Hoeksema objects that God cannot offer salvation if no salvation is there. This argument is refuted on the grounds of prescience alone. Even if God does offer salvation to all, it would be pointless providing a salvation for those who He knows will never accept His offer.

All that has been said does not exhaust the question of God's sincerity in the offer. But it shows clearly that "it cannot be proved... that there is any injustice or deception on God's part".[127]

Besides the question of God's sincerity there is also the question as to why God offers salvation to all. Some have tried to say that one reason is the mixture of elect and reprobate. This however is no reason for God, but only for man. God could certainly, if He wished, direct even the outward preaching of the Word to the elect alone (Acts 16:7–9), in which case no universal offer would be necessary.

This is not to deny that the primary purpose of God, in offering the gospel to all, is to reach the elect with the preaching of the Word and to make use of such means in converting them. For the

---

126. Calvin, *Ezekiel*, 2:248.
127. Cunningham, *Historical Theology* 2:348.

elect the purpose of the offer and the purpose of the atonement are the same.

The purpose of an offer to the reprobate is secondary. It includes the manifestation of God's goodness, benevolence, longsuffering and mercy toward him which thereby leaves him without excuse. To say though that "the goodness of God, and the offer of Christ in the gospel are His means of hardening their hearts to a greater condemnation"[128] is to distort the truth and to imply that the atonement and the offer have an intrinsic efficiency for promoting evil. The gospel may be, for the reprobate, *"the aroma of death leading to death"* (2 Cor. 2:16)—but only because he rejects it. The intrinsic value of the offer is that it can bring life (John 20:31).

Likewise the intrinsic value of the atonement is life bringing (John 3:17). No one's death was purchased by the death of Christ (Luke 9:56). In the manifestation of His goodness and the offer of the gospel God is not efficiently[129] hardening any man's heart (which would be to make Him the author of sin) but provides means that are in themselves good and useful. It is the reprobate that "hardens himself, even under those means which God uses for the softening of others".[130] If God were not to manifest His kindness, perverse man would not abuse it and he would not be further hardened (John 15:22,24). In this sense only God hardens a man's heart by the gospel.[131]

---

128. Rodman, "*The Desire of God for the Salvation of the Reprobate*", 4.
129. God fully concurs in the hardening effect of the gospel on the unbeliever's heart. It is His purpose, even if He doesn't delight in sin. But God does not efficiently (i.e. by a work of His Holy Spirit, as in regeneration) cause a man to sin, though He may use means, even rational beings (1 Kings 22:22), to accomplish this purpose.

    Sometimes the means He uses are evil (such as the *"lying spirit" q.v.*), and this can only be viewed as evidence of wrath when God has ceased in His longsuffering: see my earlier comments under "Longsuffering and Restraint of Sin". At other times God uses means which are good, as in the offer of the gospel —and these are evidence of kindness. That the sinner is then hardened in sin no more denies God's benevolence than it does His righteousness.
130. WCF 5.6.
131. We need to guard against any inference that the contents of the gospel are anything but good or that, when rightly applied, they can do other than soften the sinner's heart. The reprobate chokes on the gospel the same way as a greedy man chokes on a loaf of bread. The fault lies neither with the bread (which

There is no more I can say as to God's warrant for offering the gospel to all. Endeavouring to explain further "what is essentially mysterious, can only result in darkening counsel by words without knowledge... Such endeavours, where we have nothing to draw with and the well is deep, betray a shallow apprehension of the limits of our faculties."[132] With Owen we whole heartedly agree "is it not time for you to leave disputing and questioning the sincerity and faithfulness of God"?[133]

c) The Warrant for Our Preaching the Gospel

Having shown that we are to offer salvation in our preaching of the gospel let us now consider upon what grounds we preach.

Cunningham is surely correct when he says that "the sole ground... for men's act, in offering pardon and salvation to their fellow men is the authority and command of God in His word."[134] See Matt. 28:19–20; Mark 16:15–16; Luke 24:47–48; Acts 1:8, 17:30; Rom. 16:26.

This is not to deny that the following are relevant in preaching the gospel—first, God's delight that men would turn to Him; second, God's benevolence; third, the sufficiency of the atonement; and fourth, the mixed distribution of elect and reprobate. But none of these constitute our authority to preach.

The sufficiency of the atonement is not a warrant. "So reasoned Archbishop Ussher that though there should be boundless wealth in the treasury of the king of Spain, nothing but His invitation or permission, His 'mere good pleasure',... could warrant any poor man in taking of that fullness for his want."[135] Nonetheless there could be no offer unless there was sufficient to meet the needs of all those that took up the offer. Owen therefore describes the sufficiency of Christ's sacrifice as the "foundation" or "sufficient

is intrinsically useful for relieving hunger), nor with God (who is good and benevolent in providing sustenance, whether used or abused, Hos. 2:8,9), but only with man who abuses God's gift by gluttony.

132. MacGregor, "The Free Offer in the Westminster Confession", 55.
133. Owen, "The Strength of Faith", 52.
134. Cunningham, *Historical Theology,* 2:347.
135. MacGregor, "The Free Offer in the Westminster Confession", 56.

basis"[136] or "chief ground"[137] of "the general publishing of the gospel unto all nations". But our "commission" is only in the command of God.[138]

Neither is the mixed distribution of elect and reprobate a warrant to offer salvation to all. Nonetheless it is apparent that God does not lead us to preach particularly to the elect and therefore we "are bound to admonish all, and warn all men... giving the **same commands**, proposing the **same promises**, making tenders of Jesus Christ in the **same manner**, to all, that the elect, whom they know not but by the event, may obtain."[139] (*emphasis mine*)

Nor is God's delight that all men turn to Him our authority to preach salvation. But we should certainly preach this aspect of God's nature to encourage sinners to turn (Ezek. 18:23, 32; 33:11).

Nor is God's general benevolence our warrant. Though again we should preach this aspect of God's nature to encourage sinners to turn. It is by God's grace that He gives sinners space to repent. None who sin in this age are at once cast into perdition as was the devil. God is appeaseable and approachable and ready to bless as soon as the sinner turns. That God is not malevolent, but gracious and benevolent is evident from His kindness to all (Acts 14:17, 17:24–28).

God's benevolence is also to be our example. We are to show love to all men, as unlovely as they may be, because God does so (Matt. 5:44–48; Luke 6:35–36). We are to be perfect in the way that God is perfect, doing good to all men (Gal. 6:9–10). And if God in His *"goodness"* and *"kindness"* (χρηστότης, χρηστός) pursues their salvation (Rom. 2:4), then what greater motive have we to pursue the salvation of men? Love of God is our ultimate motive in preaching the gospel. But because we love God, we seek to be His children (Matt. 5:45) and love all men. This is our motive, not

---

136. Owen, *The Death of Death*, 185*ff*.

137. Owen, *The Death of Death*, 271.

138. Owen, *The Death of Death*,.188.

139. Owen, *The Death of Death*, 201. Owen adds "whilst the rest are hardened". I dispute that this should be our purpose in preaching the gospel, though it is not certain that Owen believed it to be the purpose of preaching either, but merely a result.

our warrant.[140]

We will therefore *"plead"* and *"implore"* others to *"be reconciled to God"* (2 Cor. 5:20), caring for the souls of men *"out of much affliction and anguish of heart"* (2 Cor. 2:4), *"warning everyone night and day with tears"* (Acts 20:31), seeking at all times to *"provoke"* men that *"we might save some"* (Rom. 11:14).

Calvin said "it is not enough [that ministers] simply advance doctrine. They must also labour that it may be received by the hearers, and that not once merely, but continually. For as they are messengers between God and men, the *first* duty devolving upon them is, to make offer of *the grace of God,* and the *second is,* to strive with all their might, that it may not be offered in vain."[141]

Paul had *"great sorrow and continual grief in my heart,"* so that he *"could wish myself accursed from Christ for my brethren, my countrymen according to the flesh"* even though he knew many of them must be *"children of the flesh"* and not *"children of the promise"* (Rom. 9:2–3,8). Yet his *"heart's desire and prayer to God for Israel is that they may be saved"* (Rom. 10:1).

O that there were such a genuine love and burden for the souls of men today. Who hesitates to pray for another in case it is not God's purpose to save him? "A minister is not to make enquiry after nor to trouble himself about, those secrets of the eternal mind of God, namely—whom He purposeth to save, and whom He hath sent Christ to die for in particular". Rather he is "bound to seek the good of all and everyone, as much as in [him] lies... and to hope and judge well of all".[142] "Because we know not who belongs to the number of the predestinated, or does not belong, our desire ought to be that all may be saved".[143] It is arrogance to try and fathom the secret counsel of God.

Let our prayers be offered up for whomsoever we have a "continual grief in our hearts", being assured that if our "heart's desire and prayer" is for their salvation, this is "agreeable to His

140. Kuiper, *God Centred Evangelism*, 98.
141. Calvin, *Corinthians*, 2:245.
142. Owen, *The Death of Death*, 188.
143. Calvin, *Institutes*, 3.23.14 quoting Augustine.

will",[144] and in accordance with that in which His nature delights.

"The obedience we render to God's providence, does not prevent us from grieving at the destruction of lost men, though we know they are thus doomed by the just judgment of God.... They are much deceived, who say that godly men ought to have apathy and insensibility lest they should resist the decree of God... The settled boundary of love is, that it proceeds as far as conscience permits; if then we love in God and not without God's authority, our love can never be too much."[145]

d) The Sinner's Warrant to Believe

What John Owen said about ministers is equally true for the searching sinner. The secret purpose of God is none of his business. The questions of election or reprobation and for whom Christ died in particular belong to God alone. These matters do not concern the sinner. His business is in the following considerations:

1. It is first of all the sinner's duty to repent of his sin and turn to God (Matt. 3:2, 4:17). As was said before this is the inherent duty of every rational creature who has rebelled against God. If there were no gospel to preach, it would still be our duty.
2. It is God's delight that men would turn to Him and be saved. He takes no pleasure in the death of the wicked (Ezek. 18:23, 32; 33:11). It is vain to speculate whether God also takes no pleasure in the condemnation of the devil, since Scripture says nothing about this. There is no written command for the devil to repent. To man alone God reveals that His nature is such that He can take no delight in the sinner's death. And this revelation is given to induce us to be converted (Ezek. 18:30–32).
3. God gives the sinner a hearty invitation to come to Him (Isa. 55:1–5; Matt. 11:28–30). By such God "makes open offer of Christ and His grace, by proclamation of a free and gracious market of righteousness and salvation, to be had through Christ to every soul without exception that truly desires to

144. WSC Q. 98.
145. Calvin, *Romans*, 335–336.

be saved from sin and wrath.... The Lord lovingly calls us off this our crooked and unhappy way with a gentle and timeous admonition."[146] Again no such offer of grace is made to fallen angels. There is no gospel for the devil. It is reserved for sinners alone.

4. God makes an earnest request to us to be reconciled to Him in Christ (2 Cor. 5:19–21). It is not just Paul that beseeches us (as a man caring for his brethren), but God Himself beseeches us, through Paul, to be reconciled to Him. "There cannot be a greater inducement to break a sinner's hard heart, than God's making a request to Him for friendship."[147] Let the sinner therefore consider this undeserved grace of God in requesting him to be reconciled.
5. The sinner should also ponder God's benevolence toward him in times past when he received many mercies and kindnesses at the hand of the Lord. He is not seeking to be reconciled to a malevolent deity who would punish him without cause, but a God who is benevolent, and who has already shown love where love was not deserved.
6. There is also God's awful command to believe on the name of the Saviour, Jesus (1 John 3:23). This command is not just a command to repent and turn to God as is the rebellious creature's duty. It is a command to be saved. It is a command to trust the Saviour.[148]
7. There is God's promise and assurance that if we believe we shall be saved (John 3:36; Mark 16:16).[149]
8. We are further assured that the blood of Christ is sufficient to cover all the sins of all that come to Him (1 John 1:7, 2:2).
9. Finally, if all the above do not soften the sinner's heart, he must also consider the dreadful damnation that lies ahead of the unbeliever. This threat is as sure as the promise, and

146. Warrants to Believe 1.1,5. *cf* Owen, *The Death of Death*, 298. The Warrants to Believe was a part of the 17th century Scottish catechetical manual, *The Sum of Saving Knowledge, and the Practical Use of Saving Knowledge*.
147. Warrant 2.8.
148. Warrant 3 *cf* Owen, *The Death of Death*, 298.
149. Owen, *The Death of Death*, 298.

its validity rests upon the same texts of Scripture (John 3:36; Mark 16:16).[150]

150. Owen, *The Death of Death*, 298.

CONCLUSION

We have now dealt with the three questions that arise from Rev. David Engelsma's summing up of the "Free Offer" issue. I have not been able to say 'yes' or 'no' to the questions as he puts them because his wording is ambiguous. Nonetheless I have made my position quite clear by rephrasing the questions in unambiguous language. The position espoused is, I firmly believe, the position of Scripture.

Both Hoeksema as well as Murray and Stonehouse claim to stand in the historic Reformed position.

Yet do either of them do so?

It would certainly be difficult to find many that agreed with Hoeksema, today or yesterday, apart from a few Hyper-Calvinists from whom he dissociates himself.

Murray and Stonehouse would seem to stand more in line with our Reformed fathers. The main difference is the ambiguity of language that they employ which is in contrast to the stark clarity that has been the usual mark of Reformed theology. Some of their more nebulous propositions could be interpreted in an Amyraldian rather than a Reformed sense.

One point has emerged from this debate. No doctrine should ever be erected on the grounds of rationalisation. I agree that Scripture is rational and that one cannot accept irrational doctrines. Nonetheless if two doctrines are not necessarily contradictory (even though they appear that way), and if both have good grounds in Scripture—then we must hold to both. We are on dangerous ground when we start to remove apparent contradictions by rationalising. As long as there is no necessary contradiction faith will receive what reason finds difficult.

Finally I plead for careful discussion and examination of this subject. It has been the cause of schism within both the Protestant

Reformed Church and the Australian Evangelical Presbyterian Church. I do not know whether these controversies were justifiable. Nor am I prepared to define what latitude of opinion should be allowed among teachers in the church. I only plead for caution and discernment.

These are not questions that can be dismissed with a few trite syllogisms, but require a thorough examination and evaluation of Holy Scripture.

APPENDIX: COMMENT ON 2 PETER 3:9

No verse has perhaps caused more contention in regard to the free offer than 2 Peter 3:9. *"The Lord is not slack concerning His promise as some count slackness; but is longsuffering toward us* (Nestle Text: ὑμᾶς; T.R: ἡμας), *not willing that any should perish, but that all should come to repentance".*

Two interpretations of this verse are offered. Both are feasible depending upon whom Peter had in mind.

1. If he had in mind an argument for refuting scoffers, his train of thought runs like this: "Listen you (ὑμᾶς) scoffers who mock the Lord's patience, you are wrong if you interpret such longsuffering as indicative of God's unending benevolence toward you. The only reason God is longsuffering is that He takes no delight in your death and is giving you an opportunity to repent before it is too late".

   Those who object that this makes God out to be waiting for what will never happen should see the explanation of the word "pursue"[1]. God's "waiting" is easily understood in the same way as God's giving *"to all life, breath, and all things... so that they should seek the Lord, in the hope that they might grope for Him and find Him"* (Acts 17:25–27).

2. Others say that Peter has in mind an argument for encouraging believers as they faced the opposition of scoffers. In such a case he is saying: "Let us not lose heart, God is being longsuffering towards those of the elect who have not yet repented. He does not will that they perish and is therefore giving them space to repent so that they might be saved and added to our (ἡμας) number".

1. Refer to page 71, footnote 93..

Calvin prefers the former interpretation, stating that the verse has nothing to do with God's hidden purpose. "So wonderful is His love towards mankind, that He would have them all to be saved, and is of His own Self prepared to bestow salvation on the lost."[2]

Owen is ambivalent, choosing the latter interpretation in *Death of Death,*[3] but the former in his treatise on *Dominion of Sin and Grace.*[4]

This ambivalence is reflected in other Reformed commentators who are not always consistent in sticking to one interpretation. Poole says Peter is speaking possibly of men generally or the elect in particular,[5] but elsewhere he refers to this verse and says Peter speaks only of God's complacential will, not His decretive will.[6] Matthew Henry seems to prefer the second interpretation when commenting on 2 Peter 3:9, but the first when he refers to this verse in Romans 10:1.

Murray and Stonehouse discuss the Greek text and come out in favour of the first view.[7] In this they are followed by R. B. Kuiper,[8] Hulse,[9] and Boettner.[10] Thomas Chalmers quotes Peter and also comments that "this continuance [of the world] is due to the goodness of God lengthening out to him [i.e. the worldly man] and to us all the season of an offered indemnity and of a proclaimed pardon, and of an inviting gospel with the whole of its privileges and blessings."[11]

Gordon H. Clark says that it is quite clear that Peter refers to only the elect, and he quotes the *Shepherd of Hermas* and John Gill by

2. John Calvin, *Commentaries on the Catholic Epistles* (Edinburgh: Calvin Translation Society, 1855), 419; see also Calvin, *Institutes*, 3.24.16.
3. Owen, *The Death of Death*, 236.
4. John Owen "On the Dominion of Sin and Grace" *Works of John Owen*, Vol. 7, (London: Banner of Truth, 1968) as quoted in Shedd, *Dogmatic Theology*, 3:424.
5. Poole, *Annotations*, 3:926.
6. Poole, *Annotations*, 3:777.
7. Murray and Stonehouse, *The Free Offer of the Gospel*, 24.
8. Kuiper, *God Centred Evangelism*, 31; Kuiper, *The Glorious Body of Christ*, 174, 181, 231.
9. Hulse, *The Free Offer*, 8.
10. Loraine Boettner, *The Reformed Doctrine of Predestination* (Philadelphia: P&R 1968), 287.
11. Chalmers, *Lectures on the Epistle to the Romans*, 1:112.

way of support.[12] Herman Hoeksema agrees.[13]

No prejudice should be entertained against the first interpretation on the basis of "frustrated longsuffering" since Romans 9:22 speaks plainly of God's longsuffering of the reprobate. However the word "willing" (βούλομαι) usually implies more than just a disposition in God's nature. Rather it suggests a definite purpose or intention; this would then point to the second interpretation. Though, regarding the cognate βουλή in Luke 7:30, see my comment on that verse under "Acts of Mercy and Kindness" on page 77.

12. G. H. Clark, *II Peter – A Short Commentary* (Philadelphia: P&R 1972), 71; Clark, *Biblical Predestination,* 140.
13. Hoeksema, *The Protestant Reformed Churches in America*, 345.

BIBLIOGRAPHY

Systematic Theology

Berkhof, Louis. *Systematic Theology*. Grand Rapids: Eerdmans, 1968.

Calvin, John. *Institutes of Christian Religion.* Vols I, II, III. Translated by Henry Beveridge. Grand Rapids: Eerdmans, 1966.

Dabney, R. L. *Lectures in Systematic Theology*. Grand Rapids: Zondervan, 1972.

Hammond, T.C. *In Understanding Be Men.* London: Inter-Varsity Fellowship, 1965.

Hoeksema, Herman. *Reformed Dogmatics.* Grand Rapids: Reformed Free Publishing Association, 1973.

Hodge, A.A. *Outlines of Theology*. London: Banner of Truth, 1972.

Hodge, Charles. *Systematic Theology*. Vols I, II, III. London: James Clarke & Co, 1960.

Shedd, W.G.T. *Dogmatic Theology*. Vols I, II, III. Minneapolis: Klock & Klock, 1979.

Strong, A.H. *Systematic Theology*. Old Tappan: Fleming H. Revell, 1976.

Turretin, Francis. *Institutio Theologiae Electicae* (*Institutes of Elenctic Theology*). Edinburgh: John D. Lowe, 1847

Historical Theology

Berkhof, Louis. *The History of Christian Doctrines.* London: Banner of Truth, 1969.

Cunningham, William. *Historical Theology*. Vol. I, II. London: Banner of Truth, 1969.

DeJong, Peter. *Crisis in the Reformed Churches.* Grand Rapids: Reformed Fellowship, 1968.

MacLeod, John. *Scottish Theology: in Relation to Church History.* London: Banner of Truth, 1974.

McNeill, John. *The History and Character of Calvinism.* Oxford: Oxford University Press, 1967.

General

Boettner, Loraine. *he Reformed Doctrine of Predestination.* Philadelphia: Presbyterian & Reformed, 1968.

Calvin, John. *Concerning the Eternal Predestination of God.* London: James Clarke & Co, 1961.

Carson, D. A. *The Difficult Doctrine of the Love of God.* Wheaton: Crossway, 2000.

——— *Love in Hard Places.* Wheaton: Crossway, 2002.

Charnock, Stephen. *The Existence and Attributes of God.* Sovereign Grace Press, 1971.

Clark, G.H. *Biblical Predestination.* Philadelphia: Presbyterian & Reformed, 1969.

Como, David R. *Blown by the Spirit: Puritanism and the Emergence of an Antinomian Underground in Pre-Civil-War England.* Stanford: SUP, 2004.

Dabney, R.L. "God's Indiscriminate Proposals of Mercy" *Discussions Evangelical and Theological.* Vol. I. London: Banner of Truth, 1967.

——— "On Fusion with the United Synod – The Atonement". *Discussions Evangelical and Theological.* Vol. II. London: Banner of Truth, 1967.

——— "The World White to Harvest" *Discussions Evangelical and Theological.* Vol I. London: Banner of Truth, 1967.

Fisher, Edward. *The Marrow of Modern Divinity* (Kindle Edition)

Flavel, John. "Sermon 12 on Heb. 10:14". *Works of John Flavel.* Vol. I. London: Banner of Truth, 1968.

——— "Sermon 1 on Rev. 3:20" *Works of John Flavel.* Vol. IV. London: Banner of Truth, 1968.

Hodge, A.A. *The Confession of Faith.* London: Banner of Truth, 1964.

Hoeksema, Herman *The Protestant Reformed Churches in America.* Grand Rapids: First Protestant Reformed Church, 1947.

Hulse, Erroll. *The Free Offer.* Haywards Heath: Carey Publication, 1973.

Kuiper, R.B. *God Centred Evangelism.* London: Banner of Truth, 1966.

——— *The Bible Tells Us So.* London: Banner of Truth, 1968.

——— *The Glorious Body of Christ.* London: Banner of Truth, 1967.

Marcel, Pierre. *The Biblical Doctrine of Infant Baptism*. London: James Clarke and Co., 1959.

M'Cheyne, Robert. *Memoir and Remains of R. M. M'Cheyne.* Edited by Andrew Bonar. London: Banner of Truth, 1966.

Murray, John and Ned Stonehouse *The Free Offer of the Gospel.* Phillipsburg, NJ: Presbyterian & Reformed Publishing, 1949.

Owen, John. "On the Dominion of Sin and Grace" *Works of John Owen.* Vol. VII. London: Banner of Truth, 1968.

——— "The Strength of Faith" *Works of John Owen.* Vol. IX. London: Banner of Truth, 1968.

——— "A Display of Arminianism" *Works of John Owen.* Vol. X. London: Banner of Truth, 1967.

——— "Of Our Conversion to God" *Works of John Owen.* Vol. X. London: Banner of Truth, 1968.

——— *The Death of Death in the Death of Christ.*

London: Banner of Truth, 1963.

(Quotations are from the separate edition, in which pages 33–312 correspond to pages 145–424 of Works of John Owen Vol. X.)

Packer, J.I. *Evangelism and the Sovereignty of God* London: Inter-Varsity Fellowship, 1967.

Rodman, Charles. *Universalism and the Reformed Churches: A Defence of Calvin's Calvinism.* Evangelical Presbyterian Church of Australia, n.d.

——— *"The Desire of God for the Salvation of the Reprobate" An ambiguous doctrine refuted and the Reformed Evangelical Church vindicated.* Evangelical Presbyterian Church of Australia, n.d.

Van Til, Cornelius. *Common Grace.* Philadelphia: Presbyterian & Reformed, 1969.

——— *Particularism and Common Grace.* Lewis J Grotenhuis, 1951.

(The 2 titles above are reproduced in: *Common Grace and the Gospel.* Philadelphia: Presbyterian & Reformed, 1972)

——— *The Sovereignty of Grace.* Philadelphia: Presbyterian & Reformed, 1969.

Van Til, Henry *The Calvinistic Concept of Culture.* Philadelphia: Presbyterian & Reformed, 1972.

Warfield, B.B. "God's Immeasurable Love" *Biblical and Theological Studies.* Philadelphia: Presbyterian & Reformed, 1968.

——— "Predestination" *Biblical and Theological Studies.* Philadelphia: Presbyterian & Reformed, 1968.

Articles

Bonar, John. "The Universal Calls and Invitations of the Gospel" *Banner of Truth Magazine*, Feburary, 1959.

Engelsma, David. "Our Protestant Reformed Position Regarding the 'Free Offer of the Gospel'" *Standard Bearer*, 1st November 1973, 15th December 1973.

———. "'Hyper-Calvinism' and the Call of the Gospel" *Standard Bearer*, 1st April 1974, 1st June 1974, 15th May 1974, 1st November 1974, 1st December 1974, 1st May 1975, June 1975, July 1975, August 1975, 1st November 1975.

———. "Key '73 - What Must We Say About It". *Standard Bearer* 49, no. 18 (1973)

Hoeksema, Herman. "Particular Throughout" *Standard Bearer,* 15th September, 1974.

Hoeksema, Homer C. "About Breaking God's Covenant" *Standard Bearer*, 15th May 1975.

———. "The E.P.C. and Common Grace" *Standard Bearer*, 15th December 1974, 1st January 1975,

———. "The O.P.C. and the 'Free Offer'" *Standard Bearer*, 1 May 1973, 15th May 1973, 15th September 1973, 1st November 1973, 15th December 1973, 1st January 1974, 15th January 1974, 1st June 1974, 1st May 1974.

———. "Question Box" *Standard Bearer*, 1st May 1973, 1st June 1974.

———. "Universal Grace-Universal Atonement-Universal Salvation" *Standard Bearer*, 15th October 1974.

Honeysett, Bernard. "The Ill-fated Articles" *Reformation Today*, (Summer 1970): 23–30.

Hulse, Erroll. "The Free Offer of the Gospel, Viewed in the light of the Marrow Controversy", *Banner of Truth Magazine*, July 1958.

Kuiper, R.B. "Common Grace" *Encyclopaedia of Christianity*.

Vol 3. Edited by Edwin Hartshorn Palmer. Marshallton: The National Foundation for Christian Education, 1972.

MacGregor, James. "The Free Offer in the Westminster Confession" *Banner of Truth Magazine,* July-August 1970.

MacLeod, Donald. "Misunderstandings of Calvinism II" *Banner of Truth Magazine,* Feburary 1968.

Murray, Iain. "The Free Offer of the Gospel" *Banner of Truth Magazine,* July 1958.

Murray, John. "The Atonement and the Free Offer of the Gospel" *Banner of Truth Magazine,* July 1968, August 1968, September 1968, October 1968.

Nicole, Roger. "Amyraldianism" *Encyclopaedia of Christianity,* Vol 1. Edited by Edwin Hartshorn Palmer. Marshallton: The National Foundation for Christian Education, 1964.

Ophoff, G.M. "Anniversary Address" *Standard Bearer,* 1st June 1974.

Packer, J.I. "The Puritan View of Preaching the Gospel" *Puritan and Reformed Studies Conference,* December 1959

Spurgeon, C.H. "Shooting the Straw Man – Confused Notions Cleared Away"

——— "Preaching to Sinners" *Banner of Truth Magazine,* March 1969.

Swanson, A. "The Doctrine of Reprobation and Its Practical Implications" *Banner of Truth Magazine,* November 1976.

Thomas, Geoffrey. "Becoming a Christian – Covenant Theology: A Historical Survey" *Westminster Conference,* December 1972

Van Dixhoorn, Chad. "The Strange Silence of Prolocutor Twisse: Predestination and Politics in the Westminster Assembly's Debate over Justification" *Sixteenth Century Journal* 40, no. 2 (Summer, 2009): 395–418.

Watson, T.E. "Andrew Fuller's Conflict with Hypercalvinism" *in How Shall They Hear?: a symposium of papers read at the Puritan and Reformed Studies Conference.* Edited by Martyn Lloyd-Jones (London: Evangelical Magazine, 1960): 22–29.

Select Commentaries and Comments

On the whole Bible:

Calvin, John. *Calvin's Commentaries.* Edinburgh: Calvin Translation Society, 1845–1857.

Henry, Matthew. *Commentary on the Whole Bible.* Peabody: Hendrickson, 1994.

Poole, Matthew. *Annotations upon the Holy Bible.* New York: Robert Carter and Brothers, 1853.

On various texts:

Fairbairn, Patrick. *Ezekiel and the Book of His Prophecy: An Exposition.* Mulberry: Sovereign Grace Publishers, 1971.

Haldane, Robert. *Exposition of the Epistle to the Romans.* London: Banner of Truth, 1958.

Burder, G. *Zeal for the Salvation of Sinners* Rom. 10:1 Sovereign Grace Union, n.d.

Chalmers, T. *Lectures on the Epistle to the Romans.* Vol. 1. Edinburgh: Thomas Constable, 1848.

Clark, G.H. *II Peter – A Short Commentary.* Philadelphia: Presbyterian & Reformed, 1972.

Fergusson, J. *The Epistles of Paul 1659–74.* London: Banner of Truth, 1978.

Hendriksen, William. *A Commentary on I Timothy.* London: Banner of Truth, 1964.

Hodge, Charles. "Sermon on 1 Tim. 2:4" *Banner of Truth Magazine,* Feburary, 1958.

Hoeksema, Homer C. "Mal. 1:2–4" *Standard Bearer,* 1st May 1973.

——— "Matt. 5:44–45" *Standard Bearer*, 1st June 1974.

——— "Matt. 23:37–39" *Standard Bearer*, 15th May 1974.

——— "I Tim. 2:1–4" *Standard Bearer*, 15th November 1974.

Watson, Thomas. *A Divine Cordial* Rom. 8:28. Mulbery: Sovereign Grace Publishers, 1972.

SCRIPTURE INDEX

INDEX OF NAMES AND SUBJECTS